# A Jersey Boy's Story

by James Thomas Walsh

Copyright © 2024 by James Thomas Walsh

ISBN:   978-1-77883-489-9 (Paperback)

All rights reserved. No part of this publication may be reproduced, distributed, or transmitted in any form or by any means, including photocopying, recording, or other electronic or mechanical methods, without the prior written permission of the publisher, except in the case brief quotations embodied in critical reviews and other noncommercial uses permitted by copyright law.

The views expressed in this book are solely those of the author and do not necessarily reflect the views of the publisher, and the publisher hereby disclaims any responsibility for them. Some names and identifying details in this book have been changed to protect the privacy of individuals.

BookSide Press
877-741-8091
www.booksidepress.com
orders@booksidepress.com

# Contents

Introduction ........................................................................................... 5
Chapter One: The Quest April 28, 2003 ........................................... 7
Chapter Two: The Master's Plan ...................................................... 14
Chapter Three: Miss Colvin ............................................................. 16
Chapter Four: First Communion ..................................................... 20
Chapter Five: Big Black Cloud ........................................................ 22
Chapter Six: Mrs. Kresge ................................................................. 30
Chapter Seven: Frank Gallager ........................................................ 32
Chapter Eight: Wildwood ................................................................ 34
Chapter Nine: Mr. Ross: Science Teacher ...................................... 35
Chapter Ten: The Day The Music Died ........................................ 39
Chapter Eleven: Cars ....................................................................... 42
Chapter Twelve: Sister's Tricks ....................................................... 45
Chapter Thirteen: Mike Flora's '32 Ford ....................................... 48
Chapter Fourteen: Seventeen—Joanne—The Time of My Life ....50
Chapter Fifteen: "The Times They Are A Changing" ................... 53
Chapter Sixteen: Skid To A Stop .................................................... 62
Chapter Seventeen: Meet Louie ...................................................... 72
Chapter Eighteen: Darkness Falling ................................................ 74
Chapter Nineteen: The White Sportster ........................................ 89
Chapter Twenty: Roxanne ............................................................... 98
Chapter Twenty-One: Double Crossed Twice .............................. 101
Chapter Twenty-Two: A Crumpled Piece of Paper ..................... 141
Chapter Twenty-Three: Sister Celeste .......................................... 147
Chapter Twenty-Four: Boca Raton ............................................... 151
Chapter Twenty-Five: Hold On To Your Seet Terry Bomar ...... 155

Chapter Twenty-Six: Muscles ...................................................... 157
Chapter Twenty-Seven: John Defendis ....................................... 159
Chapter Twenty-Eight: Still Horny After All These Years ............ 170
Chapter Twenty-Nine: Ezekiel .................................................... 180
Chapter Thirty: Boca Hotel Murals ............................................ 186
Chapter Thirty-One: Art institute ............................................... 190
Chapter Thirty-Two: Time To Move Again ................................ 192

# Introduction

*"Ask and it shall be given you, seek and ye shall find, knock ant it shall be opened unto you." Luke 11:9.*

Much of life is lived as an unsolved and convoluted mystery where clues briefly emerge like dreams in the night and disappear as mist.

In September of 1996 I was struck by a truck while driving my Harley motorcycle. I was near death several times and after three and a half years in a wheelchair and thirty-nine surgeries over five years I was able to walk with one leg five inches shorter.

I began writing this story in 2003 in an attempt at self discovery, to find out who I am and why I am still alive. Though much of the content is a chronology, the events are really the background and material from which I have formed and tested my being and beliefs over my lifetime.

The story you are about to read is an autobiography. All the events are real and accurate without exaggeration. The people are real though many of their names have been changed as well as the locations of some events.

*Chapter One*

# THE QUEST

## *April 28, 2003*

"There are no coincidences." Ric Wynn affirmed after about fifteen minutes into our meeting at his office on campus.

I was fifty-one years old, heartbroken, ashamed of myself, and not knowing where else to turn when I called Ric. Among other things Ric was teaching Psychology at the County College of Morris where I had completed my Associates Degree. He and I often talked at the Power House Gym near the school where we both trained.

After an hour's attempt to unwind the knotted thread of thoughts and emotions that I spilled, Ric challenged me to write down the story of my life beginning with my earliest memories and to look there for the clues.

This in essence is it; if my memory serves me correctly:

My earliest memory is seeing the sun. It was spring time, the lawn was fresh, and the sun was hot. I wondered what it was, so bright in the sky. My dad told me not to look directly at it because it could damage my eyes.

I also remember Christmas. I would turn four in January. My dad lined up six orange and white boxes with blue lettering on the living room floor. The first had a beautiful .027 gauge red caboose. The next contained a black coal hopper car, the next a silver 'Sunoco' liquid container car. Then out came a green barrel car. Next was a black coal tender, and finally from the longest and heaviest box I struggled to remove the engine! Engine number 2055 would receive the name *Smoky*, and my sister Sharon and I would chant "Two-o-five-five, two-o-five-five, *Smoookee!*" to the rhythm of the wheels and the long toots of the whistle.

My track was already set up inside the oval on which my brother John's train ran along with the little town called *Plastic Ville*. I had the church, the airport and a gas station. John had the train station, the firehouse and the hospital.

John was almost three years older than me and he got his Lionel train set at his first Christmas. He still has it today. My train was my best gift ever. I loved the smell of the engine. We would pack them back in the original boxes and open them up the following Christmas for many years. I often set my train up and the little town throughout the year and imagined what it could be like to drive the locomotive. What happened to 2055 Smokey took thirty years. Smokey was the only childhood treasure I kept guarded into my adulthood. Hidden safely in the original boxes packed in a closet in my mother's attic in the house I grew up in.

Thirty three years passed since I first opened those wonderful orange and blue Lionel boxes. I had now been married and living in a School building on Pompano Beach in Florida and teaching art in trade for our third floor apartment over my second floor studio, both having beautiful ocean views.

My sister Sharon was now divorced from her first husband and she lived with her son Joey and our mother at the house in the lake where we grew up. On this particular family visit back to Jersey I had an inclination to check on my friend; Ol' Smoky. The boxes were the same, the cars were the same, everything even smelled the same! The sense of smell has amazing subtle power; it triggers emotional memories with precision. Ask any mechanic what his favorite smell is, or ask any woman about fresh linens or her children's hair. Once the scent of that machine oiled engine got in my pores I was forever a man with tools.

By now there was no room in the small house to set up the track and test the train out so I brought the set into the garage where I had built so many motorcycles in the past, and set a sheet of plywood on two saw horses and connected the track. Carefully I removed each car from its box as I always had being watchful not to damage the car or the box it came from. I plugged in the transformer and flipped the red toggle slowly and the whistle came to life! Next I slowly advanced the black throttle switch and watched the headlight begin to glow and the engine said "Grrr" while the steel wheels turned and the push rods chugged. We took a slow cautious lap around the track carefully watching for any flaws that might derail the locomotive. Joey who was ten or twelve at the time joined me as I gave Smoky increasing doses of power explaining the dangers. Smoky was as perfect as that first Christmas Day some thirty years ago. I politely asked Joey not to touch the train if I wasn't around explaining how precious this gift was to me. He agreed and I locked the garage.

Two days later we were all gathered around Grandma's kitchen table having lunch with a friend of Joey's and I thought I would prank the kids by saying "Who messed with my train? I found it crashed!" But when I saw the look in their eyes I realized it was no joking matter. Joey had gone with his friend into the garage without my permission and derailed Smoky scraping the paint and breaking a small green light off of the engine.

I was hurt and furious! But this was my sister's kid. So I approached Joey man to man only to have him sneer at me and say, "So what is the big deal! So what if it's an antique! Who cares anyway?"

Well, he's not my kid so I didn't smack him. I sucked it up and my sister told him he would have to earn the money to repair the train. Smoky went carefully back in the boxes and was returned to his safe hiding place in Mom's attic and I returned, a little heartbroken, to Florida.

I anguished in prayer over my loss for a few nights and this answer came to me as a voice saying, "I had something that was perfect too, and I cared deeply in my heart for thirty three years as well, and my precious one was disfigured by those that did not care or understand. So tell me Jim, what are you going to do about it?"

The next day I picked up a World Vision flyer from my dining table that asked for help to feed orphans in Africa. I had no money but I had a solution. I knew the kid was never going to fix the train unless someone pushed him, and it wasn't going to be me. No, when I visit Mom the next time I'll fix Smoky as best as I can myself. Then I'll sell him to a collector. I'll take all the money from the sale of the train and send it to World Vision to care for the kids in Africa. My train probably wouldn't do them much good sending it there; these children needed food and probably had no electricity to waste. If I do this for the One that lost something very precious as well, maybe I could actually give Him joy. Joy that His loss was not in vain, and joy that other children that were precious to Him were not forsaken.

That's what I did.

I make it a habit to check my closets for clothes and things I'm not really using. I challenge you to today to look around and see what you have in boxes or under tarps, or somewhere safe, it doesn't have to be precious; maybe just forgotten, you don't have to take a risk, most of us have too much stuff. Give something away. It will come back, one way or another.

Hey, I got a train to catch!

My next childhood memory is my dad burning my teddy bears. Actually he made me throw them in a bon fire of leaves we raked up in the yard. At four years old he thought I was too big to have teddy bears. He never hugged us. Neither did mom. At least I can't recall one incident.

Raking leaves proved to have a positive turn as well. A few short years later I recall raking the oak leaves in piles and paths around the yard into a kind of Grand Prix track. Viewed from above with a little imagination it appeared like red mountains and canyons seen from an airplane or an eagle's eye. As I raked the leaves I imagined being a race car driver taking treacherous turns.

Next I was in an airplane surveying the terrain below. But most euphorically, I was an eagle, soaring, diving, watching and guarding my turf as I reveled in the glorious freedom of skillfully flying with superior wings!

As I was raking leaves and imagining these things my father approached with a booklet in his hand. "I thought you might like this." he said as he handed it to me. It was titled, *On Eagle's Wings*. My father worked as a bookkeeper for a small local trucking company close by. He also belonged to the Fraternity of Eagles, and he kept the books for a local chapter. That's where the booklet came from.

The title, *On Eagle's Wings,* was actually a quote from Isaiah 40:31 and the booklet explained the Ten Commandments. That booklet had a profound impact on my life. I felt exhilarated reading it out there in my yard! I spoke to God and He listened to my heart. This was a truly divine moment, one I would seek to recapture time and again. It was rare, precious and elusive.

## *History*

'*John E.J. Walsh*' sounded like a title. It was my father's name. He was known by his peers as *Honest John*. Yeah. That says a lot, and it was all true. I admired his character and was proud of him, though I feared his presence all the years we were together.

John E.J. was the second oldest of five children (four boys and one girl) born of James Thomas and Mary Walsh, a typical Irish catholic family of civil servants living in Orange, a city slightly west of the ports of New Jersey. My great grandfather was the Police Chief, grandfather James Thomas Sr. was the city Fire Chief. His first son, James Thomas

Jr., became a police corrections officer. All the brothers served in the military during WW II. Genevieve the youngest child was James and Mary's only daughter. Their history is an Irish tale. My grandfather died before my brother John and I, and my little sister Sharon Ann were born. Apparently my grandmother died when I was a baby.

My mom was another story: *'The Secret life of Ceil'.* Sufficient to say, Cecelia S. Wisneiski was a coalminer's daughter. She came from a family of ten, and yes, her father was a Pennsylvania coalminer. He died of 'Black Lung' disease long before we were born, and Grandmother was gone before our time as well. They only spoke polish in their home. Only the children were bi-lingual.

My brother, myself and my sister all came into this world by cesarean section and none of us were breast fed. My mother used to tell me that when she was supposed to deliver me that she lost a lot of blood, had gone into shock and received a number of whole blood transfusions, so my delivery was postponed for two weeks while she recovered. We all often pondered over the years what was in that blood. Did it influence my nature?

In December of 1952 Dad and Mom, my three year old brother John and I; now eleven months old, moved from the city of Orange, New Jersey to the little rural township of Parsippany Troy Hills in a small Cape Cod home that sat across the street from Hoffman Beach, one of four beaches on the mile long lake named after the Lenapee Indian tribe native to the area. Most of the homes in Lake Parsippany were converted bungalows and several log cabins that once were used as summer retreats for city folks. It was a poor man's subdivision of lots and blocks carved out of woods and farmland. Newer permanent homes began to spot fill in as time proceeded and the last dairy farm faded away from the higher ground with a few remaining colonial mansions. Mom missed her city life and viewed Parsippany as a "God forsaken place" that she would have to put up with, adjust to, and eventually call her home never desiring to leave.

My sister Sharon Ann was born on May 14, 1954 and along with my brother John, we three kids learned to swim, fish and ice skate across the street from our home. I found solace gazing out of our living room picture window and watching the lake glisten and the ducks and majestic swans make their rounds.

*Chapter Two*

# THE MASTER'S PLAN

The 1950s post WII era was an idyllic time in America where roles were clearly defined as well as enemies, and on both sides of the iron curtain atomic bombs were being tested. Although Parsippany seemed like a jungle to city folks, it was only a lazy thirty three miles from ground zero; New York City, a likely target for a nuclear strike. All over the nation people were building bomb shelters, television ran national broadcast tests and schools drilled in preparation for an attack.

Tucked into our elementary childhood years was my father's master plan to improve our basic Cape Cod home into a humble and secure castle, and he would have had us dig a mote if our childhood lasted long enough to complete it with our servile labor. For now he was intent on busting up the concrete slab in the crawl space that the house rested on and dig out a bomb shelter basement from the clay earth below. No he hadn't worked out the drainage problem that would ensue when "water seeks its own level" neither was he too concerned with health issues, child labor or other details. He was right about one thing though, "Discipline, discipline, discipline." He constantly assured our mother that we weren't being tortured, until she learned to reply verbatim "As the twig is bent, so shall the tree grow."

You would think he learned the concept of child rearing from a concentration camp. We all watched tons of WWII movies, and Dad did serve as a Staff Sergeant in the U.S. Army in the Philippians. I'm sure that stint supplied his booming voice with plenty of practice for my brother John and me to deal with when we arrived.

Our job also included digging a shallow pit about a foot deep, against the north side of our house the size of a one and a half car garage and fill it with stones screened from the clay dirt brought up in hundreds of wheelbarrow loads out of the "Hole" as the pit under the house came to be known. This stone filled space was then capped off with cement and was used as a summer patio. We also became masons adding a waist high cinder block retaining wall along the west side of the patio. The remaining screened dirt we spread over the entire yard.

You would swear the "The Great Escape" was filmed there, and that Hollywood got the whole plot from my brother John.

Yeah we learned discipline there. We also learned anger, and, we got stronger as our blisters calloused. My brother became huge while learning to control and channel his rage boiling within. His size supplied me with a buffer from my dad, and his control taught me to wait and strike. By the time dad passed away my brother John had fist fighting honed into an art form using his anger like a precise cannon sight backed by two hundred pounds of dynamite. This was good. It gave me time to think.

The digging went on for years until we knocked a support column out from under the house cracking a beam in the attic and had to jack the house back up with a post. That took a little smoke out of "Mein Kamp." And by now Dad had political aspirations.

*Chapter Three*

# MISS COLVIN

As children we didn't have very many toys, but fortunately my mom handed me some paper and pencils when I was four years old, and as I lay on the living room floor I began to draw Disney characters, Mickey Mouse and Donald Duck. The drawings astonished my parents and everyone that viewed them.

Like all great men my father had flaws, but he had sterling attributes. In particular he had vision. Nowhere in my family's history on either side was there a hint of artistic talent. No one could draw even a stick figure, but my blossoming talent was obvious, and Dad had the foresight and good sense to do something about it. He called in a local artist to review my drawings. While my sister and brother and I played on the living room floor, Dad and the artist passed sheets of drawings back and forth. As the artist studied each figure his eyes would lift from the pages and he would study my brother John. Finally, lightly tapping the drawings in his left hand, he gestured to my brother and enquired of my father, "You mean to tell me that this little kid made these drawings?"

All eyes widened as my dad replied, "No, not this one, the younger one."

"This is remarkable! You better get him to school. You better do something for him" the artist replied.

The next year I entered Kindergarten. My teacher's name was Miss Colvin. She was young and beautiful with lovely dark hair and a most pleasant voice. She showed me where the blocks were to build something with, and I made lot of new friends. We joyfully ate graham crackers with milk and then took a nap on our little rugs we brought from home. As nature would have it, I really enjoyed talking softly with the girls lying next to me.

Miss Colvin told us to ask our parents to give us an old baggy shirt or 'smock' as she called it, to bring to school to cover our good clothes while we learned finger-painting.

The smell of the paint and the glossy paper were overpowering and wonderful to me. For the rest of my life I would have affairs with paint fumes. We dipped our fingers in the gooey paint and began making squiggly designs. We quickly discovered that a child's hand print looked very much like a turkey. And the index finger could make puffy clouds and trees and the yellow sun with protruding rays.

There was something about my composition that intrigued Miss Colvin. "I would like you to try to make a painting Jim." she gently spoke in her soothing voice.

I smiled and nodded and Miss Colvin took my hand and walked me to an artist's easel.

Then she opened a large pad of painting paper and clipped it securely to the easel. We gathered up small cups for paint and water that fit snuggly in the easel's tray, and then quite proudly, Miss Colvin produced several paint brushes with very long handles. Some were pointy, some were flat, and some were almost round at the tip!

"Jim what would you like to paint?" she asked with a smile.

"An airplane in the sky" I replied.

Once upon a time on a warm summer Saturday, my visionary father took our family to Hanover Airport which was one town over. The airport was surrounded by woods and fields, and a junkyard close by. It accommodated prop planes, mostly single engine Piper Cubs and biplanes, and a couple of twin engine propeller driven planes as well.

Mom was too afraid to go up, and my sister was too small to appreciate the ride, but my dad paid for the gas, and his friend Burt

Dodge, the pilot, took my brother John up first. It was a beautiful sight! When they returned the pilot waived my dad and me over, my brother was glowing! We climbed in exchanging seats and taxied along the bumpy unpaved runway.

Gaining speed as the woods approached, we left the earth and the bumps and the woods behind, and I learned that day what eagles know. Some call it ecstasy, some: living perfectly 'in the moment,' others; an epiphany. The experience would remain with me for ever.

To the glowing eyes of Miss Colvin, Burt Dodge's single engine Piper Cub was flying off the page!

That evening my father got a call from my teacher. He greeted Miss Colvin and cautiously inquired what the matter was about.

Miss Colvin began by explaining that, "The class was finger-painting today and Jim was not…" But before she could continue with "only" Dad interrupted pensively, "Oh that's odd, my son likes to draw."

"He is not only painting with his fingers, he is painting pictures with brushes! Beautiful, accurate, detailed pictures, far more advanced than any kindergarten student. I'm calling to encourage you to nurture his exceptional talent and to consider art lessons for Jim."

My dad took the admonition seriously and in a few years he found an art teacher perfect for me.

Dad had been volunteering his services with the Lake Parsippany Property Owner's Association making sure the life guards had their First Aid requirements in order with their kits and safety equipment, and making his presence known. He also started the local Democratic Party with Vince Sapanore and himself as the first two members. In little time he was nominated by the party to run for the position of County Clerk which he lost to a majority Republican vote.

Dad recovered from the loss by refiguring his master plan for the home and contracted two local carpenters to add an open car port over the patio slab and retaining wall. There were lots of scraps of wood lying about from the construction which I collected along with bent nails which I carefully straightened, and having quickly grasped the intended uses of a hammer, I built an entire village of custom ranch homes to enhance my model car collection.

After a couple of weeks though Dad began to complain about "the junk in the yard" and made me destroy my subdivision. It broke my heart, but I obeyed.

*Chapter Four*

# FIRST COMMUNION

At seven years old a Roman Catholic child prepares to make his First Holy Communion.

Those of us in public school are required to attend Catechism classes to learn the basic tenants of our religion. It was scary! Priests and nuns covered up in black pointy costumes that have the power to hit you! And then there's Jesus' life-sized emaciated marble white and blood stained body sagging on a wooden cross reminding me of the severity of God.

Hell would be much worse! And even your sinful thoughts could send you reeling into its darkened torments! I tried with all my might not to picture naked girls. I would start singing something immediately, or recite Our Fathers and Hail Maries and Glory Bees…but mostly I would quickly shake my head to rid the thought. I could hide in the bathroom and pray on my knees later where no one would see me and think I was crazy. Maybe I could find absolution there.

The real test would come in the confessional. Children making their First Holy Communion had to be at the church on Saturday at a specific time to confess in turn. My parents made me late! Father Boss, yeah, that was his name! Father Boss reprimanded me for being late when he heard me recite, "Bless me Father for I have sinned. This is my first confession." That was an emotional scar.

The next test was not to have any bad thoughts until at least, after you received the Communion wafer on Sunday! A dirty thought was a mortal sin, and if you didn't go back and confess it to a priest and then took communion, you were guilty of the mortal sin of sacrilege! I lived in constant fear and trembling each time I left the confessional until the communion was over on Sunday. For the next ten years I battled alone for control of my mind and control of my nature, sharing this with no one.

In first grade we learned to read and print. In second grade we learned to write in script; cursive writing! While carefully copying the beautiful curving letters from above the chalk board onto light green writing paper, the 'in ecstasy-epiphany' returned to me like the anointing of the Holy Ghost; Perfection in the present moment, if it was possible. I touched it with my mind, my eyes beholding, my fingers guiding my pencil point in between the bold pair of lines divided by a lighter line that indicated the height of the lower case letters. Once again I was flying like an eagle.

My teacher Mrs. McKenna recognized my beautiful penmanship, and, I believe, my euphoria as well. She smiled from the front of the room, and walking over to me asked, "Jim, how beautiful! You are doing great! Would you like to help some of your classmates with their letters?"

It was that feeling of perfect stillness, a time stopping, mid–breath beautiful moment that would return throughout my life, usually when I completely forgot it ever existed, that connection with the supernatural that gave me faith and made me want to live and be a good human for the sake of a grander purpose.

*Chapter Five*

# BIG BLACK CLOUD

Seven years old was a crossroad for me as an Irish Catholic boy. The wooded lots between our homes served as playgrounds for boys where we learned to build forts and identify Poison Ivy plants. We took breaks from our labor and held pissing contests which I won all the time. There were wild grapevines that we eventually tried to smoke, and black raspberry bushes in abundance where we stood and ate the juiciest fruit and talked for lengths of time on end identifying Robins and Blue Jays, and the more exotic Baltimore Orioles, Scarlet Tanagers, Golden Finch, Red Winged Black Birds, Red Headed Wooded Peckers and Cardinals both male and female.

Jerry DeCroce was my closest friend, both by proximity and interest. His mother was my mom's best friend and they lived cattycornered across the street from our back door.

### *Cousin Marty's 1958 Corvette*

My cousin Marty, who is fifteen years older than me to the day, he and I have always had two other things in common, our love for cars and girls. Whenever he showed up he had a new one of each. In the spring of 1959 he showed up with a black and silver Corvette with red leather interior nicely complimented by a blonde named Lynn who danced with the famous "Rockettes" chorus line. What a sexy car!

Some day I have got to get one. In the meantime I got into building and customizing model cars and dreaming of becoming a teenager and getting my driver's license. Jerry and I were definitely on the same page here and often I would walk over to his house with a couple of my latest car creations and we would play on the floor burning rubber and driving around with our make-believe girlfriends as we listened to the latest hit songs on AM radio. Jerry had a big sister; Maryanne, who was three years older and beautiful, and kept us informed of all the latest teenage trends.

Another Italian American couple with three sons our ages lived across the street from Jerry, and around the corner was the Ecke family of seven. We were all friends most of the time. At least I thought so until the mettle got tested.

Billy Ecke who was my age was hanging at the stop sign on the corner with Jerry and when they saw me walking, called me over. Billy could not wait to tell me this off-color rhyme he and Jerry learned the day before as Johnny Malise joined the group.

"Johnny is a friend of mine
He will xxxx me anytime
For a nickel, for a dime
Fifty cents for overtime!"

They all laughed and explained what exactly it meant pointing at each other substituting names and threatening to fight over the insult.

Having recently made my First Holy Communion I found this actually disturbing. I smirked nervously and dismissed the thought of any serious discussion. After all they were my friends, even if they were a little stupid sometimes. Instead I chose to leave the group and headed home.

Somehow their folly was overheard that same day by Jerry's dad and he became furious at Jerry, so the boys quickly reconvened and created a plan to keep Mr. De Croce from reading the riot act to their own dads.

Of course I wasn't there to hinder their progress and naturally became a convenient scapegoat to be buffered by my older cousin Marty.

The remaining boys Johnny and Billy found me again on the street and explained that their story was that my cousin Marty; who was now twenty-one and driving cool cars and dating, had visited and taught us all the rhyme. Marty was way too big for anyone's dad including his own, to give him a beating, and he lived in East Orange, untouchably "out of sight and out of mind" they thought.

Not liking this plan I turned my steps up Jerry's walkway and knocked on the front door. Sam, Jerry's dad came to the door and pointing his finger in my face began shouting loudly his accusations and disgust, and threatened what he would do to me if I were his kid. I began to shake with emotion and fled home to tell my dad what happened. My dad asked me truthfully, did I teach this thing, to which I promised "No." My dad knew me and he knew that Marty hadn't been around recently and was not going to let Sam De Croce get away with abusing his son, so he took me by the hand and we walked swiftly over to the De Croce's and knocked on the door. Jerry and I waited silently in the living room while my dad and Sam talked this out with increasing volume in the kitchen. Mrs. De Croce, my mom's best friend began crying with less and less restraint until she was yelling at her husband how stupid he was while Sam turned to yelling at Jerry for lying.

Dad and I left settled, and Mrs. De Croce called my mom apologizing for her crazy husband's behavior. Mom accepted her apology calmly but would not call Teresa again. Silently their beautiful friendship ended, and though I saw Jerry in his yard occasionally we never again met to play with our model cars and sing rock and roll. By choice I didn't bother with the other guys either and Jack Kiernan and Chris Kopp became my new friends.

For now there was Janice Burnham. She was my classmate during our elementary years and her back yard conveniently butted up against Jackie Kiernan's yard with whom I would walk to school every day and eyeball Janice through the corner of my eye as she strolled a parallel path to our nearby school. Janice had a crush on Bobby Accardi who lived up the hill in the newer and better split level homes. As children we already began to feel the effects of social class separation. Bobby and Janice had that sweet relationship all the way up to our freshman year of high school. Jill Birch liked me and by fourth grade Colleen Hawkins was my dream girl, but I wasn't getting close enough to hold hands with anyone for years to come.

I still had to go to catechism classes until I made my Conformation when I became twelve years old. Then I could stop attending the classes. Somewhere between the two Sacraments, as the Catholic Church called them, I think it was the summer between my fourth and fifth grade in school, I found my classmate Tommy Harrison staggering around in his white shirt and pants in and out of the lake at the beach across from my home. I think it was Sunday because I went home and got my father. He assessed that Tommy was drunk and carried him to our house and put him to bed on the living room couch explaining that Tommy was sick and would be vomiting. Tommy fell asleep and I did what I thought a believer should do. I knelt next to the couch and prayed for my God to save Tommy's life. Tommy awoke now and then and heard me pray. He puked, a lot, but he lived.

My dad was there again to rescue Billy Ecke one time when Billy came around the block at full speed on his bicycle and couldn't quite make the turn at the bottom of Laurence Road. He crashed into the neighbor's picket fence and flew over the handle bars nuts first. Man, what a scream! My dad ran and scooped him up and never stopped running until he got Billy into his parent's arms. He lived too.

I don't remember praying that time, but I do remember praying a lot; before every meal, after every meal, and before going to bed. My dad taught me to pray before I went to sleep. I can remember asking him what I could say at night while praying and the example he gave me I still recall word for word. I understood early on that I should pray certain learned prayers, and that I should talk to God in my own words as well. There were years when it became an obsession that some would call an obsessive compulsive disorder. Whatever you call it, I was tangled up with fear and I handled it by trying to meet God and please Him in prayer.

## Girt English and the Gaffe Rigged Sailboat

Somewhere in the foggy memory of those childhood years lies a grey wooden rowboat with a red bottom leaning against the back side of our house. I vaguely remember that my dad and my brother John took it out fishing on the lake one day. It needed regular maintenance that it got only once so we used it as a fort most of the time. Across town lived an elderly widow named Girt English; she was thin and very plain and always wore black. My father would do occasional chores for her around her home without asking for any compensation, but he did have his eye on an old wooden sailboat in her yard that needed a lot of fixing. Naturally one summer Girt gave the boat to my dad. Dad got his friend Vincent Sapanore and his teenage son Vinny to haul it home and strip it down to the bare wood and together they refinished the boat beautifully with a varnished mast and wood trim.

When launching day came I was told that I was too young to sail in that magnificent craft and would have to watch the maiden voyage from the shore line. Dad, Mr. Sapanore, Vinny and my brother John tacked that majestic vessel with its huge square main sail and triangular jib across the lake brilliantly. They came about catching a bundle of air and she healed starboard as the crew hung out over the windward portside to keep her up. I watched the foam break at the bow and a long wake trail behind. It was exciting, beautiful and awesome, like a clipper on the ocean.

The very next weekend Vinny asked my dad if he and a few of his teenage friends could take her out and my dad happily agreed. The wind was strong that Saturday and the boys worked hard to handle the ship. I watched from our living room window as the sky darkened and the trees began a steady sway. A summer storm had come from the north and was blowing unrestrained toward the lake. Being situated on the north shore, the rain spattered on our housetop before reaching the water and my picture window quickly became spotted with droplets as I stared out at the straining sailboat. Lightning cracked and thunder bellowed as the boys frantically drove her into the wind to make it to the shore before the next bolt lit the lake, but the tall wooden mast was a lightning rod and the storm struck her like an electric sword. I watched amazed as the mast snapped in half with a terrible crack and the sails crumbled and fell.

The boys made it in with no one hurt, but inside my chest my heart was bruised along with the others. The wooden mast could not be repaired and to replace it outweighed the costs. She never sailed again, but like Marty's Corvette that sailboat created in me a goal I would seek to fulfill over and over with future boats.

The next summer my Uncle Frank; Marty's dad, was cleaning out his place, and he dug out an old wooden canoe that was skinned with canvas glued on with some kind of black pitch and then painted with battleship grey enamel. The paint was horribly cracked and the canvas dry rotted, but underneath the wood was good. Uncle Frank offered it to my father and I believe he accepted it because he saw the heart I had for the sailboat that I had never experienced.

Dad and Uncle Frank leaned the canoe up against the oak tree in our yard and covered it with a tarp. With Uncle Frank's instructions Dad showed me how to strip clean the wooden hull and told me that the boat was mine. That felt good.

He explained that my brother John had the row boat, but because he didn't want to take care of it, it became junk. Now was my turn.

I spent the whole summer and early next spring hand stripping that canoe when my father had a change of plans. Dad wasn't going to finish the canoe, he didn't really have the skills, and I think he wanted to spare me the torment of another one of his laborious projects gone array, so he suggested that we put a "For Sale" sign on the project boat for the handsome sum of ten dollars, and when it sold, I would get the money.

I agreed really because I had no choice. Even then ten dollars did not seem like much compensation for the labor I had already done, or for the loss of a dream, and in reality it was not but Dad was trying to make good.

In a short time an auto body repairman from up the street bought the hull and covered it in fiberglass, painting it red and varnishing the wooden insides and rub rails. It was lovely.

Years later when I attended County College I took sailing lessons for gym credits in a one man "Sunfish." I saved some cash a bought a "Sailfish" which is the cheaper version. I kept it on our lake for two years and out grew the challenge. I few years later I met Roxanne at her yard sale. My sister's husband Mark grew up a few houses away from Roxanne and informed me that she had a fourteen foot Comet for sale along with an off road motorcycle. By this time I had been building, showing and riding custom motorcycles for many years so both were of interest to me. I headed over on my trophy winning Sportster to show off my wares and charm her into giving me a deal, but when my eyes beheld her exotic beauty I was caught like a deer in the headlights! This lovely woman was a mix of Philippine and German and belonged on a beach in Tahiti with a flower in her hair. My very first thought was "She will look this beautiful when she is fifty." Truthfully the artist in me then saw the timelessness of her God given captivating beauty, and as I am writing these pages more than thirty years later, should you behold her today you will agree with certainty, I was right. Everyone who knows her agrees, "She is beautiful!"

So I show Roxanne my bike explaining that the custom storybook paint job is my work, to which I hear her reply sarcastically "Yeah right!" and have to resort to pointing to my signature hidden in the details, claiming that if she takes me on a tryout sail in her boat I'll take her for a blast on the bike, it would only be fair. All the while my head is composing time alone with her captive in the saddle on a romantic country tour that should take just the right amount of time.

So with perfect sunlight bouncing between the trees and sparkling on the water, and with a cool summer breeze on our faces, I cruised at a comfortable speed and talked to her cheek to cheek in my mirror. Then when the right moment came I turned my head and landed a kiss that changed our future forever.

I never did buy her old boat or trail bike, but sometime later I gave Roxanne a diamond ring. Within a year we bought a seventeen foot "Islands" racing slope that we had for a few years. I still dream of having a world class yacht the size of a ranch house to escape to.

*Chapter Six*

# MRS. KRESGE

By nine years old I was considered an artist prodigy and my wonderful dad found a private art teacher for me. Mrs. Patricia A. Kresge, wife of Gene and mother of three, gave me the fondest education of my life. For the next five years she would teach me, one on one, how to draw and paint with pastels and later in oils. She and her family loved the country and loved horses. Their home bordered on a reserve of woods. Pat was spellbinding in every good sense of the word. She was a beautiful woman of about thirty years with a perpetual disarming smile, lovely long and wavy chestnut brown hair and crisp blue eyes. Her voice would always capture and soothe my soul, with a gentile cadence that carried me to the warmest parts of being alive. Under her watchful eyes I kept on course, while her beautiful hands taught mine to move with precision and grace. That angel of art surrounded me with creativity. I listened to her with all of my soul in attendance. Only then was I comfortable in my own skin, free from anxiety.

In August the Morris County Fair met at the Grange Hall on South Beverwyk Road which had a well-attended and respected art competition. With Mrs. Kresge's encouragement I entered the competition and won first place in the junior class for pastel painting. The junior class was for artists ages zero to twelve years of age. Four years consecutively I won the juniors under her tutelage.

Every Christmas I set up Smokey and my train set. I had my art lessons, and I had my other love; building models, especially model cars. Boy I loved cars! When Dad would ask what I wanted for Christmas I always said a model car. Somehow he didn't understand that but he complied, usually reluctantly. I suppose things might have been different if he had spent time with his children, perhaps teaching us sports like other fathers did, but that didn't happen and we were never really attracted to playing any sports. I became embarrassed though as I grew older and was not skilled like my peers, but I had my personal internal life customizing cars and dreaming I'd be a rock star and a hero.

For now I was happy finding a stray dog I named Blackie, a medium sized mutt in a wavy black coat. My father reluctantly allowed me to keep him if I would care for him which I did. In fact I was the only one that could go near him. Eventually my dad had enough after Blackie bit my cousin Johnny on his already injured arm. Blackie never had shots or a license or anything and my dad wasn't up to getting a lawsuit so he told us that he was taking Blackie to live on a farm where he could run. I believed him.

*Chapter Seven*

# FRANK GALLAGER

Thus my enlightenment continued. Frank Gallagher stood like a dark obelisk, six foot three inches tall with thinning grey hair and tight straight lips, and though he wore glasses he could watch a fly scratch his name on the head of a pin at twenty yards. Mr. G was no less than a renaissance genius and a perfectionist, with a red hot temper and a booming voice. He frightened everyone, even the school principle. He seemed a little like Hitler to us eleven year olds. He was also our hero reflecting the noblest virtues. Mr. G was a math genius, an English master, and music aficionado with a most discerning eye for art. He had a perfect ear, perfect grammar, perfect penmanship and perfect manners, and insisted on the same from us all. Mr. G taught it all to us with great discipline, clarity, and love. He was a middle aged Irish catholic bachelor who whipped the blackboard with a pointer and slammed desks on the floor when he was angry, and he through candy buttons and other treats to the class when he was pleased. He was an amazing storyteller, an unmatched teacher and an unforgettable man.

When Mr. Gallagher taught us the math portion of our studies he gave extra credit in the form of military rank for solving increasingly difficult problems that he kept top secret for each level. Along with having arrived at the correct solution, critical emphasis was placed on alignment of numbers in columns, penmanship, page format, and cleanliness. Erasure smudges were not acceptable. It could take several drafts before handing in the final paper or you would receive a different problem of equal value to gain the desired rank. Breaking class rules at anytime was assigned demerits and you could lose you rank for such behavior.

He was the strictest teacher, but you wanted to please him more. You earned his praise and he matched your joy. He was kind and fair and protected the weak. I learned how to listen and how to learn from Mr. Gallagher. I learned more from his teaching than I did for the next seven years of my required public education. Many of us were doing math at a twelfth grade level in his fifth grade class as we listened to his private collection of operas like Aida and master composers like Mozart and Beethoven. He opened our awareness to the minds of Leonardo D Vinci and Michelangelo, Daniel Webster and George Washington, Albert Einstein and Trauntinburg as we sang Christmas carols he taught us in Latin. Mr. Gallagher fed our brains and they grew larger under his care, from the best to the least of us he was fair to all.

Mr. G asked one favor from me. To decorate his wall above and the length of his blackboard with an original mural of *The Sparrows Returning to Capistrano*, on a roll of paper he could keep for ever.

I met him by accident a dozen years later and he reminded me that he still possessed that painting I made for him. He believed in me.

*Chapter Eight*

# WILDWOOD

By now my father had begun taking us on a one week vacation to the sea shore town of Wildwood New Jersey where he rented an apartment a few blocks from the beach. The quaint three story building was owned by the O'Connor's, another Irish family from our home town of Parsippany. O'Connor just happened to be my grandmother's maiden name. Whether that influenced Dad or not I do not know, however he saw the area as an opportunity and began immediately looking for a similar apartment building to invest in as well. A realtor, Mr. Dare, located an old but immaculately keep place about a mile north and only two blocks from the beach. It was also a three story building with six apartments, and it also had a smaller two story apartment building to the rear on the east side that the owner's stayed in. On the west side stood a fairly new golden brick Catholic Church. Dad closed the deal in 1964.

*Chapter Nine*

# MR. ROSS: SCIENCE TEACHER

## *1964 World's Fair for a Painting*

## *First visit to Stokes State Forrest*

My seventh grade science teacher Mr. Ross recognized my artistic talent in the beginning of the school year and took me aside to explain that he had the foresight to capitalize on my genius. With that Mr. Ross offered to take me and a friend of my choice for a day outing at the World's Fair that was being held this time in New York City, all expenses paid. My friend John McNabb and I could see any sights we liked and take the tours and rides of our choice. On the top of our list was to see the Ford Motor Company's new Mustang being introduced and sit in the cars as they traveled through the historic display of the motor company.

Mr. Ross had two conditions. The first was that he wanted a painting from me, using whatever medium and subject I chose. The second was that I must see Michelangelo's Pieta which was brought over from Italy for viewing at the World's Fair. Naturally I complied.

For a seventh grade boy sitting in a brand new Mustang convertible as it rolled through history was awesome, but even that experience was muted by the incredible life of this marble statue. The muscle tone, the hands, the veins and the limp exhausted body of a tortured innocent in the helpless arms of an agonizing mother, so still so cold and yet so full of emotion, both gripping and helpless, the deed that marked time and marred perfection carved and hammered in vulnerable stone so soft and clean like bruised lips in the peddles of a lily speaking life from death in magnificent silence.

"It is said that if you look carefully, her hand quivers." Mr. Ross whispered.

Time stopped. I held my breath for the whole tour around that perfect work and silently vowed to return the blessed favor to Michelangelo for talking to my heart. It was an epiphany, what I now call a "Selah" moment, like when Mrs. McKenna saw my face and felt my glow as I slowly lettered the alphabet in script for the first time. A feeling as if a white dove quietly landed on my shoulder and rested a moment then took flight only to return unexpectantly years later again and again.

Mr. Ross took our whole class on a field trip that spring to Stokes State Forest; a fourteen thousand acre track of pine woods with an intoxicating smell and beautiful brooks winding in a ravine made for fairy tales. Stokes became a place I would escape to often for most of my life.

That year I made out with a dark haired girl named Bobby in a red and white striped blouse at the junior high dance. I liked it. That summer I discovered that if you walk around the lake you can meet girls. I met Annette Bravo, but she had a boyfriend. That was okay because I met Bettyanne Fenareu. We loved kissing by the lake. It felt so good, so strange and wonderful, my heart pounded with excitement. My world became more complicated.

It was 1965 when my Father accepted the nomination from the local Democratic Party to run for the Mayoral seat in our home town.

That summer I saw a color television for the first time in a repair shop across from our old elementary school, and that same year the Kresge family moved to the greener pastures of Pennsylvania, and I lost my angle of art for ever. Dad didn't lose his sight for my art career, even with his huge campaign he made arrangements for me to meet with another well acclaimed tutor, Mrs. DeBlique. Now age thirteen, I had to move up to compete in the senior competition at the Morris County Fair against people that painted for a lifetime. Under her guidance I won first place in oil painting that year along with my first place pastel painting of *The Arabian Horse*.

Five blue ribbons in five years should give me a clue as to what I should do with my life, some insight to my purpose, but I did not see my future.

Three months later my Dad was elected Mayor of Parsippany Troy Hills. In January of 1966 he took the oath of office in the auditorium of my junior high school. We were ecstatic. The whole ordeal had been parallel to the election of John F. Kennedy to the United States Presidency. Both John Walsh and John Kennedy were handsome, charismatic Irish-Catholic Democratic underdogs in their forties, and this was the nineteen-sixties. It was magical, and "for one brief shining moment" it was "Camelot."

It was so good that I got the courage to ask him for an electric guitar for my birthday, and I got it! I got it with the speech about how I was going to pursue practicing diligently and not just get tired of it and put it aside after he spent all this money. I thought I proved myself by then because he gave me a cheap Sears's acoustical guitar the Christmas before last and I took a few lessons from my brother who was given a guitar plus lessons two years prior but had bailed out. From then on I taught myself to play it as best as I could without any professional guitar lessons. I didn't need the heat from Dad. He was scary enough being nice.

I knew that this new electric guitar and amplifier I got were the cheapest in the store, that wasn't bad, just knowing we were born poor people was humiliating. That unspoken judgment and rejection from better families might have vanished if Camelot could have lasted a while, but it didn't.

*Chapter Ten*

# THE DAY THE MUSIC DIED

Eleven months later on October 12, 1966 my father and encouraging patron; Mayor, John E.J. Walsh died from heart failure at age 45. Five fire trucks full of flowers that emptied the florists in three counties accompanied the motorcade. There were three twenty-one gun salutes from the United States Veterans, the Parsippany Troy-Hills Police Department, and the Federal Order of Eagles. "Taps" played and an officer handed my mother the flag, folded in military ritual, from Dad's coffin. We had one more thing in common with the Kennedys, our hero was gone forever.

Every opportunity that may have come our way vanished like smoke. The dream was over as quickly as it had come. Abandoned by the powers, we were socially and economically poor again.

My brother John was only twelve days away from his seventeenth birthday when our father died, and because Mom did not have a driver's license, he was able to get his quickly. Mom relied on him to get her to the grocery store, but she never went anywhere else except to work with a lift she took from a woman co-worker.

I never entered the Morris County Fair art competition again. The light I painted by went dark for years. I was lost, alone, depressed and afraid.

My mother shut down emotionally. She went to work and meagerly managed the bills. The town did not have a life insurance plan in place for my father and there wasn't any pension or compensation when he died. Incredibly there was no mortgage insurance on the newly purchased Apartment building in Wildwood either. This mystery remained until her decease in 2002. Our primary residence in Parsippany was only $5,900 when my father purchased it in 1952, and his old check book showed that the house payment was about $150 a month, so whenever he could he would make a double payment leaving us with a small balance which his mortgage insurance paid when he died.

When I turned fifteen that January 19, 1967 my cousin Marty gave me his Vespa motor scooter with my mother's hesitant permission. She justified it by saying that she believed that I was more level headed than my brother John who was denied permission to buy a motorcycle because of the many possible dangers attributed to riding, and really because my brother had a propensity to be a bit wild in her mind.

I fell in love with the feeling of riding. It was like learning how to fly. Ask any biker and he'll tell you, you either get it or you don't. I got it! That Vespa changed my life forever!

Mom was however adept at manipulating and she managed each of us in turn to get things done for her. I was always the maintenance man. My brother John, who was now a licensed driver, wanted no part of spending his summers in Wildwood caring for the apartment building. He agreed only to drive Mom, Sharon and myself there to clean, paint and do repairs while he partied at home in Parsippany with his teenage friends. Then he would come back for us.

Sadly for me, while I was being the good son, my brother John took my beloved Vespa without my knowledge and with his reveling friends destroyed and discarded my precious ride.

Mom having no recourse sold the apartment building for the debt balance at the end of the summer of 1968. Lacking the strength to guide or encourage us, or teach us how to grow up and survive; she pulled the shades, locked the doors and shut out her family, her friends, and the world completely for the next 37 years with little improvements until she passed quietly in her Parsippany home at 82 years old.

*Chapter Eleven*

# CARS

My brother John, perhaps seeing the error of his ways, brought home a 1946 Chevy panel truck which he promptly gave to me as a project custom. Within a week he arrived with a huge 409 cubic inch Chevy hemi engine that needed rebuilding and added it to the offering. I spent two whole summers sanding that truck down to the bare metal with a high school classmate Mark DeGroat, and dreaming of making it into the coolest hot rod until Mom decided it was an atrocity and demanded that it be junked. I had no choice. That was a heartbreaker like the teddy bear and the sailboat, all that working toward a dream and now someone in charge tells you that you can't have it, "Period."

So like the canoe before, all that labor of love dreaming I would have something was like skin stripped off of me.

I think that all along Mark had more motivation to help me on the truck than that of just being my friend. My sister was a young long legged, blue eyed Irish lassie that had a mane of auburn hair spilling off her shoulders which he got a peek at every day that that old truck crouched in our yard.

My sister Sharon made up her own mind and began to date Mark DeGroat.

Brother John had purchased a 1956 Buick Special from Vinny Sapanore and cleaned and polished up the two tone metallic blue and silver paint to a luster, but by the summer of 1967 he had sold it before you knew it and bought a light blue 1958 Chevy Impala convertible with a white top. It came with the powerful 283 v8 and power glide transmission, but John saw to it that it would have a more powerful camshaft which he and his buddy installed right in the yard.

The muscle car era was in full swing and it wasn't long until he sold the '58 Impala and bought a 1964 Chevy Impala Super Sport with a 300 horsepower small block, a four speed, and a 4:11 posi-traction rear end. Jeff Kennedy the owner, was getting married and it was time for him to sell his bachelor toys. He purchased the car brand new and kept it in showroom condition. It had a rare paint scheme consisting of a white body with an aqua metallic roof. The seats were rolled white leather, buckets in front, and the dashboard, floor console and carpet matched the aqua roof. John decided it was a little too tame and began taking it to Sedgfield Gulf up the road and had the Benson brothers crank up the horsepower. A set of 375 Fulie heads and solid lifter cam plus a dual point distributer got things rocking while Hooker Headers and dual quads completed the top end. It turned into a monster! Cups and glasses would shake in our kitchen as he idled the car into the garage. Eventually he traded the dual quads off for a better mixture with a huge Holly on top of an Edlebrock high rise manifold. Pairs of one hundred foot streaks of rubber marked Big John's turf in town.

One morning as John was leaving the house he discovered that someone had broken into his Impala SS and stolen the floor console. The police came and did their thing but could not prove anything so John did his own investigation. What he discovered was that his friend Sammy Gaskill had just bought a console from Sid Peer that was painted black. Further investigation showed that underneath the black paint was the console's original aqua color. Coincidence?

Sid peer was the owner of a 1963 Burgundy Impala Super Sport on which he just spent a huge some of money having the engine professionally rebuilt with gobs of goodies. Sid was claiming that now he had the fastest car around. So John decided to go see Sid and his

43

pride and joy and Sid was thrilled to show John his car.

"Let's hear this hot motor!" John prodded Sid. "Rev it up!"

Sid, happily complied and started up the car. As the solid lifters began to tap, John urged again, "Rev it up!" and Sid complied.

It only took a minute for the lifters to loudly clack and with the hope of increasing the oil pressure Sid gave her another large gulp of fuel. The clacking ended with a bang and the engine seized to a halt. When Sid pulled out the dip stick he discovered that there was no oil in the motor. The dry engine welded itself to death.

"Man, you should've checked the oil!" John said hiding a snicker. Apparently someone had snuck up on Sid's car the night before and drained out all the oil into a pan so there was no puddle under the car, replaced the drain plug and disappeared into the night.

John's next undertaking was to enclose the carport that attached to the house and turn it into a garage that he could lock his car in. I gladly assisted.

## Chapter Twelve
# SISTER'S TRICKS

After dinner I would meet up with the boys and we would walk the streets looking for something fun to do. My sister Sharon met with her girl friends and they pretty much did the same.

One evening Sharon, Barbara, Paula and Teresa thought it would be fun to tie a fishing line across Lawrence Road and hide while some unsuspecting driver snapped the line with his windshield. My friends Chris and Jack, and myself had just happened to be passing the fishing line when two teenagers from Morristown who were out cruising for girls, turned the corner onto Lawrence road in their 1954 pink and gray Ford. The girls were hiding, but we were right in the open when the Ford snapped the fishing line with a loud crack. Knowing we would be blamed the three of us ran through the yards and between houses to escape a beating from the older teens.

We got away that night and the girls had a good laugh, but the two guys in the pink Ford weren't going to give up that easily. Night after night they returned cruising the town on the lookout for me and my pals.

After a week passed my brother John asked us from who or what we were hiding from every night. Both the girls and the guys together gave Big John the story and he decided it was time for him to get in on the action. He loved to give out a beating and he could justify this one.

Our house was on the end of the block with Lake Shore Drive

running along the front yard and Halsey Road running behind our house lined with large oak trees and a setback of tall hedges. Intersecting the two parallel roads was Lawrence Road.

John allowed the girls to hide in their usual spot to observe, and placed my friends and I visibly on our corner where Lawrence Road and Halsey Road connected while he crouched down behind us near the hedges.

John told us to choose a few good sized stones for defense to fit in our pockets while he himself dug up a basketball sized boulder.

The pink Ford coming toward us on Halsey slowed to a crawl as it entered the intersection with the two boys inside it hoping for trouble. They got it. When the car cleared the intersection John stepped out and hurled the boulder onto the trunk lid of the '54 Ford with a thunderous boom! The boulder cratered the lid like the face of the moon as the driver nailed his brakes screeching to a halt behind our house.

"Who threw that rock?" the tall blonde driver yelled defiantly opening his door.

"I did!" John returned pushing the rest of us aside. "What are you gonna do about it?" he demanded and softly instructed us to circle toward the passenger's side in case he got frisky.

But seeing John and seeing us, the passenger; a large two hundred and forty pound black man, pointed his index finger into the air and exclaimed "Let there be just one fight!" and closed his door.

John grabbed a fist full of the driver's shirt while he was still seated and yanked his head two or three times against the roof and door pillar. The driver eventually tumbled out of his car and rolled between two oaks and the hedges into the poison ivy that liked to trail up the trees.

John dropped one knee onto the guy's gut and began pummeling his face and head with his fists all the while explaining the consequences of hunting his brother and his friends to him. Mom was inside the house and hearing all the racket ran out our back door and approaching the scene began to yell "John stop! You're gonna kill him! John! John!

You're killing him!"

By now John's fists were getting bruised so he switched to banging on the guy's head with his forearms until he figured the guy had enough and maybe Mom was right, so he picked the guy off the ground by the back of his collar with his left and with his right hand grabbed the rear of the guy's belt and slammed him twice headfirst into the driver's side door. The door, hanging damaged on its hinges swung slowly open with a squeak and John threw the driver back into his seat as the roof of the car caught his head one more time. He learned his lesson. In fact, the very next weekend Blondie showed up in the day light and when he saw John and me nailing shingles on the garage he ran into the yard and picking up the dropped nails was offering to help!

Eventually John reunited with his junior high school sweetheart, and following in Jeff Kennedy's footsteps he sold the Impala Super Sport and purchased a new milder 1969 Chevrolet Impala Custom.

*Chapter Thirteen*

# MIKE FLORA'S '32 FORD

By now it was becoming obvious that I was pretty handy with tools, I think partly because of the love I had for hot cars, that I was always building models and got the principles down. I had hands-on experience with the Vespa and I was always the family handyman. John and I with a couple more guys put a new roof on Mom's house before he moved away, and he and I closed the carport into a garage after the break-in. I alone had replaced for mom all the cabinets in the kitchen, upper and lower, along with all the plumbing and flooring, and papered the walls adding new trim as well. Along with my growing skills was an increasing collection of tools.

A kid named Mike Flora lived only a few houses away, and being his father's namesake, Mike senior bought Mike junior a 1932 Ford three window coupe! Wow! Young Mike was only fifteen and had two younger brothers. Their father worked for the town road department and they were as poor as us but their family all shared a love for cars and this was a father and son project. Mike senior could weld and had an engine hoist built into his garage. In no time he had a big block Chevy engine with gobs of horsepower squeezed into that simple Ford frame. Young Mike didn't have a driver's license yet but his father let him burn rubber up the driveway all summer. We could hear it blocks away. It was earth shaking! I would stop by weekly to get the latest update on the car's progress when Mike began telling me that they were going to get a new black paint job on the rod and I should be sure to check it out.

One fine day Mike Flora came jogging up to my garage with a copy of *Hot Rod Magazine* rolled in his hand. He opened it to the centerfold and showed me a custom car with a sunset over a lake painted on the vehicle with a spray gun called an *airbrush*. The whole article was just one paragraph but I got "the picture." Now I hadn't drawn or painted a thing since my dad died, but everyone still knew me as the artist prodigy. Little Mike Flora put my life back on track with these words, "You can do this, right Jim?"

"Yeah I think so…but I don't have an airbrush."

"Can you use spray cans of touch up paint? I'll buy lots of colors of touch up paint."

"Yeah, that ought to work."

With that I sprayed a sunrise on the trunk lid of the rod and began a ship on the door but the tape kept pulling the art off. I learned a lesson on paint preparation and compatibility from that first effort.

Mike Flora and his family were more than pleased and so was everyone that saw Mike's car. I bought my first airbrush and a sears air compressor with a regular spray gun and business began.

*Chapter Fourteen*

# SEVENTEEN— JOANNE—THE TIME OF MY LIFE

When I turned seventeen things began to look up for me. I got my driver's license, bought a '57 Chevy for $75.00 that I dragged out of an overgrown lot, and, I met the love of my life. Joanne was fourteen-going on fifteen and went to school with my sister Sharon. Like me, Joanne was an Irish-Polish Catholic and the middle child of three. Unlike myself, she had two sisters and her parents were divorced. Her mom was the Irish one who had a skinny younger boyfriend named Freddie. Joanne and I went steady. We had our imaginary wedding and exchanged vows in the car while we were both losing our virginity together. It was almost, God forgive me; *holy*. We made love all the time after that.

I had a job in Mario's Record and Tape Shop and made tapes and installed eight track tape players in cars. Joanne would visit me after school. The summer of 1969 came and went as I worked with my friend Jimmy Hawkins for the Town Recreation Department. I got us both the job there on my Dad's name and my brother's reputation as he was working for the town Water Department. By Augusts' end I got my motorcycle license and bought a 650 cc 1956 Triumph Thunderbird from a guy called Pumpkin who lived locally and was moving up to a Harley Sportster. It cost me $350.

I entered my senior of high school and hung mostly with my buddies Jimmy Hawkins and Beauy McGuire. We graduated in June of 1970 and I took my beautiful Joanne to the prom and got to sleep together for the first time that night.

Beauy got his girl Debbie pregnant and the families agreed to let them marry though they were so young. They moved to Pennsylvania and dropped out of the picture. Roger Young bought a BSA motorcycle and took Beau's place for a short while. He showed me how to mix and sand body filler and we painted our gas tanks in Frankie's garage near my home in the lake.

Graham Scheyer was a good buddy to Roger and we soon became great friends. Graham was a bit shy socially because he was different. Fully grown he was maybe five foot seven or eight and weighed 138 pounds fully dressed. He grew a full unkempt beard and always wore farmer's jeans. He was a silversmith by trade and his passion was everything old including his 1929 model A Ford pick-up truck. He drove around in a Land Rover when muscle cars were the rage and he lived in a cabin in a rural northwest part of New Jersey. The access road to his cabin was a private farm road that first passed an old decaying stucco mansion in the woods that had cement lions on the overgrown porch and the whole thing looked like the "House of Usher". It made trips to see Graham exciting especially bringing a girl or someone new there for the first time at night and especially if you smoked a little pot. Graham loved smoking pot!

After two years together Joanne became pregnant and we decided to tell her mother and ask permission to marry. Her mother was furious and adamantly refused forcing Joanne to have an abortion and demanded that we never see each other again. We were painfully hurting and deeply in love. I threatened suicide and drove to the waterfall in the Boonton Basin where we used to go together, where I had carved

"Jim and Joanne 3-28-69" into a large rock to immortalize our union. It still remains there today.

This time I climbed the falls. Peering down I knew I wasn't going to jump but I was angry and would at least protest vehemently. They were taking away my bride and my unborn baby.

I was talked down by a police detective and taken to the local jail. In a few hours I went before a judge to determine if I was a threat to myself. Still angry I told him I didn't know what I would do. His Honor decided that I needed a night in the county jail to get a perspective. He was right. I was released the next day and no charges were ever filed.

Joanne and I found ways to continue to be together for another year without detection until her older sister Dianne threatened Joanne and finally ratted her out to their mother. Unexpectantly her mother decided that if this relationship was strong enough to continue under these past circumstances than it must be genuine and she permitted us to continue together.

For a short while I worked in a gas station under an alcoholic boss named Smitty. I got my first car loan and bought a three year old Cutlass coupe with low miles on it. Then I quit working for that abusive man. I didn't like any adults after that and never wanted a boss again.

*Chapter Fifteen*

# "THE TIMES THEY ARE A CHANGING"

When my sister Sharon, who was two years younger than I, reached seventeen she became the next taxi for our mom since our brother was escaping the family ties. Brother John married his high school sweetheart Carol Certisimo on October 24th 1970. More and more John's life began to distance him from Sharon, Mom and me, but he had honestly turned his life around, bought a home a few miles west of our home and began his family. He moved again to the west side of Jersey while he worked for New Jersey Bell Telephone, then transferred out to New Mexico where invested in a small business eventually leaving the phone company he had worked for in both states and developed his own business and lifestyle. John and Carol had three daughters in all. And although we saw little of each other from then on, Big John remained my hero until his passing in 2010 at sixty years of age.

Acid Rock replaced Motown Music. Long hair and bellbottom pants replaced the razor cut and Italian knits. Smoking pot was "in". Pot was huge, easy to get and cheap.

I had become a hippie artist by trade, air brushing images on vans and motorcycles as well as turning wrenches. My garage became the coolest place to be, a landmark for decades and generations of bikers.

My home town had a tight network of friends. Everyone was "cool." Everybody smoked dope but we all kept it to ourselves. There were no rats or big mouths. It was part of the code and everyone understood it. You had to be cool.

I started smoking pot when I was 18. Kids in town started much earlier, like my friend Joey, he started at twelve. Joey, then sixteen, hooked me up to my first joint. He explained that I could buy joints at two or three bucks each or I could cop a nickel bag which was five bucks, hence the name, sell two or three joints off, have two for free and make a dollar profit besides. I took the option. Joey was a good buddy, he knew the ropes. He learned early from his older brother and his brother's friends. Next he hooked me up to Timmy and Pumpkin. They were both twenty years old, two years older than me. I already knew Pumpkin having bought my Triumph motorcycle from him.

Incredibly, these long haired hippies were so typical they could have been Cheech and Chong! They drove a Ford Econoline van and wore granny sunglasses with bell bottom jeans and cotton smock shirts made in Mexico, on cooler days they wore ponchos.

Timmy and Pumpkin routinely drove that van right to Mexico and filled it with kilo bricks of Mexican Mary Jane. Yeah, they put a couple of shirts and ponchos in the truck as well for cover. It was an incredible time in American history. Easy Rider was our summer movie.

Timmy and Pumpkin set up shop temporarily at Sharon Stolman's little cottage at the lake. An ounce of weed was fifteen dollars wholesale, twenty retail. I could buy a pound of grass for eighty five dollars, and I did. It made sense. Sixteen ounces at fifteen bucks minimum equaled two hundred and forty bucks, minus the original eighty five, and the net profit came to at least one hundred and fifty five dollars! That was a whole lot of money for an eighteen year old kid in 1970. They weighed it out on a spring style hanging grocery scale. The deal got even sweeter. I could buy a whole kilo (2.2 pounds) for $135.00! Of course I did. They liked doing business with me, I was smart with plenty of business savvy, and I had lots of close knit friends, and that was safe.

You had to have guts to ride a motorcycle back then. Riding meant you were already labeled an outlaw hippie druggie. I rode. So did my pal Hank. We called him "Head." Not just because he was one, (a term applied to a pot smoker) but also he had a huge one. He had charisma and was funny as well as strong in mind and body. Guys gravitated to Hank. We both had Triumph motorcycles at first and with our girls on back, we were the only two bikes passing each other in a spring snow storm that year. In some ways we thought alike. Hank wasn't afraid of anything. He had a confidence that made us love to be around him. He connected me up to the Jersey City boys. We moved some Hashish around. Then brown Colombian pot came into play. It cost more, $315 to $ 325 a pound, but it was worth it. It smoked so much better and there were a lot less stems, and, you could sell an ounce for forty dollars. It came smuggled in on freighters into the ports of New Jersey and New York. You know who controlled that.

## *Broken Brake Rod*

I sold my Triumph motorcycle to Jimmy Hawkins for $650 and bought my first Harley- Davidson from my high school auto shop classmate Richie Tietz for the same price. Nice dealing! I joyfully recalled that Tietz had rolled the Harley into the school hallway on our last day of school and pulled a hole-shot burning rubber as he exited the school rear door. He never got caught. Now it was mine! A 1946 knucklehead ridged frame jock shifter with a suicide clutch and no front brake, and if you nailed the rear brake the linkage would let go because the threads were so worn down on the adjusting rod it would slip off when you needed it most. Only the coolest dude could start one up like this, let alone ride the thing. You needed to be a good Harley mechanic and have a huge set of balls. Both came natural to me. I earned the right and everyone knew it.

I used to take a short test cruise every time I lit her up favoring back roads hippy style and surfacing in the finer neighborhoods deliberately for the effect, and also dreaming of the day I'd have a home like that and be accepted again into finer society. I'd tease myself hawking out the beautiful society teenage girls, give a wave or stop and talk until someone's dad walked out and gave the stare. The girl would put her hands on her hips upset with her dad and I would disappear back into the wild.

Leaving one such neighborhood put me at a quarter mile straight run, though a little bumpy, up to a stop sign at a must turn "T" intersection, and then onto the main drag toward my lake. The traffic was light on that strip and it was often used as a testing ground for motor heads to express their skills and leave their marks, but it was safer going away from the "T" intersection because you had some room to decelerate than heading toward it where you met the instant stop. But I wasn't going that way. I had just changed the drive sprocket on the transmission output shaft allowing for higher revs during rapid shifting to gain increased acceleration form a dead stop and this was the perfect place to test it out. With this set up I should be able to get all four gears quickly reaching a hundred mph, and have enough room to brake and down shift safely up to the stop sign.

I rolled out of the nice little subdivision and aimed straight for the sign. I cracked open my throttle in first, jammed it into second gear wide on the throttle, jammed into third still hard on the gas, slapped her into fourth for a second and a half, and shut the throttle closed while leaning on the brake pedal carful not to lock the rear wheel and skid out of control. The sign was coming up fast as I pulled the shifter down into third and let the clutch grab. The bike shuddered and growled angrily as I pressed the pedal hard. The stop sign was still coming at me fast and a big brown UPS truck was heading into the intersection unaware of this torpedo coming to broadside her. With one hand on the throttle, the other on the shift knob, my right leg pushing down the brake and my left leg hanging over the clutch pedal, I pressed the brake for just a little more, but the brake rod let go and the linkage slipped off! I lost the brake. Time slowed to a crawl and sound disappeared. Everything but my thoughts was now in slow motion. I watched to see if my life would flash before me as so often one hears can happen. Big Brown, the stop sign, and I were all fighting to be in the same place at the same time, and that time was quickly becoming NOW! I yanked the shifter into second and opened the throttle while leaning my body weight hard to the right with my eyes measuring the space between Big Brown and my left handgrip, and the stop sign's edge and my right handgrip. It was in the mail! I just squeezed through the hole and now was powering up to stay ahead of the lion's mouth. A shift into third and I had acquired two car lengths and was breathing, but now I needed to make a left turn and head down a steep hill that also ends with a "T" intersection and stop sign. This time I'm heading straight into the lake if I fail to stop. Fortunately I'm not going a hundred mph this time. The engine is my brake from here out so down into second I go turning down the hill toward the water. Down into first and the motor painfully complains while I search for my hidden ignition shut off switch as a last option. No need, no one is there and I make the turn easily now I can slowly trot in second gear around the lake to my home a mile away. Finally as I get to the home stretch, the last two blocks on Lake Shore Drive, I hear and see the families enjoying the beach across from my home. I take another good gulp of air and relax into a smile and just as I lean her left into my driveway I see the garage door closed and remember "I have no brakes!" I jerk her to the right and miss the garage by an inch but not the garbage cans! Mr. Cool made another fabulous entrance into the world of rock star sitting in a pile of peas and corn and yesterday's dinner smothered with gas and oil, and a little pride.

## *Meet Casey, and Blow the Motor*

On one lazy August day I rolled the Knucklehead to the level street in front of our house and gave her a couple of priming kicks to pull some fuel into the carburetor before flipping on the ignition. The engine rolled over two turns and stopped with a tiny squeak. That's almost never good. Springs can squeak but this machine had very few springs. Yeah there is a pair in the front forks and a set of four in the valve train but this motor had solid lifters and the seat sat without springs right on the frame. Also this 1946 model frame was a factory ridged. That means that there was no shock absorbers to squeak at the rear wheel. No, I think that squeak is a ring rubbing in the front jug. Or maybe it is nothing. "Nothing" is easier to fix; cheaper too. Now, I could roll that big beast uphill into the garage and begin to spend a month unbuttoning the motor, or, right now just crank down on the kicker again and verify my hearing.

The decision was really simple; proceed. The gas station was about a mile away. If the bike lights up as usual I'll go gas her up at Sedgefield Gulf, roll away from the pumps, and relight. The worst that could happen is a rod bearing freezing because the oil pump is older than me, and the motor lets go. I love this machine but I know she is a ticking time bomb for a rebuild. Either way it is going to come apart soon. Maybe I'll just get a nice little ride today.

She lit up fine. I took her easy to the Gulf gas station, reached down between the rear cylinder and the drag pipe and flipped off the ignition. Not the factory location for a switch, but this was a bare bones bike. It had only five strands of wire running the lamps and the motor. I didn't even use a key, just a toggle switch that the prior owner installed out of sight. No one really would attempt to steal this guerilla and ride off with it anyway. Everyone recognized it and most people were clueless as how it worked, plus it wasn't something you could just toss in the back of a pick up too easily.

Casey stood six foot four inches at the pumps. With black wavy hair combed back and deep blue Irish eyes, he was the quintessential handsome bad boy. His smile dazzled. His voice hypnotized girls and scared the boys. We became friends right then and there. It was a mutual respect and a friendship that has lasted a lifetime.

# "The Times They Are A Changing"

The Benson Brothers Owned the gas station. Earl was the elder and he ran the business like a businessman. Bobby was the younger and he was cool. Both had tremendous talent turning wrenches and they built race cars for the drag strip in competition with other service stations, and hopped up the local street muscle cars.

Earl was in his office and Bobby meandered out of the garage to catch the show while Casey changed my dollar for gas. I told him about the squeak and my solution. He grinned. This would be right up his alley.

"I'll roll out onto 202 in first gear and twist the throttle" I told Casey "Then I bang second gear and if she stays together I'll be riding today. If she doesn't, home's not that far."

He nodded in agreement as I set the kicker. Again my knuckle rumbled back to life and I curled up the kickstand with my left foot and dropped onto the seat. Then I leaned her weight over to my right leg and stepped on the clutch with my left foot using my left hand to slap the jock shift into first gear. Route 202 was clear both ways and I was pointing north. Casey left the pumps and walked toward the road with Bobby casually in tail to see the show. When my tires were straight on the good tar I hit the gas and she roared to life. With a quick left step and hand jerk into second she roared to a peak and exploded apart. In that instant my forward connecting rod broke as the piston froze in the front cylinder launching the jug up into the frame under the fuel tank. The bottom half of the connecting rod still on the crank swung like a hammer ripping through the engine case exposing the turning crank and leaving a hundred feet of oil and metal fragments down Route 202 as I disappeared in a sideways tornado of blue smoke. Both plugs were still firing and the motor was running on the rear cylinder while I grabbed the clutch so the rear wheel wouldn't lock when the rear cylinder seizes, and I gently rode down on the back brake so I didn't skid on my own oil that was pouring back onto the tire. Gas and oil were firing out of the holes with each pulse of the plugs and my pants were hot but I got her to the roadside, threw the kickstand down and leaped to the shoulder. For a moment I watched her running on one jug at idle, on fire, with the crank exposed. So I timed the pulses, reached in and flipped the ignition switch off.

Following the debris trail in my line of sight, my eyes came to rest on three tall men in mechanic's uniforms staring back.

"It's a hot day for pushing." I thought as I humped my smoldering craft toward home.

By the time I reached Casey still grinning from ear to ear "You should have rode her home." he announced, since the motor refused to die. Bobby was standing behind him trying not to grin while Earl maintained his famous tight lip hands on hips posture, but we all had laughing eyes.

Boys will be boys.

I decided to go to the County College while I break down the Harley and do a complete make over on it during the colder seasons. I had to make this rebuild all my handiwork. Jimmy Hawkins began to work for Mario full time at the new record and tape shop at the K-Mart Plaza on Route 10 in Dover, and he got a little one room apartment a couple of minutes up the road. The County College was only a few minutes further up Route 10 and it all made a nice little package for a short while. I stopped at the record shop on nights that Jimmy worked and he would give me the key to his place for Joanne and me to be alone. But the romance for Joanne and I was fading. College opened up a new enthusiasm for life for me. I also met girls from so many different towns. My horizon expanded. I met a thin dark eyed girl there named Liz with an incredible head of chestnut hair. Our hormones got the best of us immediately. Sadly I said good-bye to Joanne, my first love, and embraced the newness of spring coming to life again. Yet for the rest of my life I questioned that decision.

As I disassembled the bike I cleaned the parts inspecting everything for wear and usefulness and labeled jars for the nuts and bolts. The parts went into boxes accordingly which were then neatly shelved while those parts to be chromed were packed for traveling with a duplicate list. I made a wish list of new parts and began stripping the paint off of the original ridged style frame.

When spring came I brought the frame with a new rear fender and Sportster style fuel tank to my friend Dennis McCarthey's house; also in Dover across the street from Jimmy Hawkins' place. Dennis guided me with the body filling, priming and base coating with a cinnamon colored paint. Then the parts returned home with me to do my airbrush work. On the top center of the tank I laid down a golden sun with radiating rings and overlaid this with a nutmeg colored silhouette of a young couple in a standing embrace. The nutmeg followed along both flat sides of the fuel tank making a mountain range and several small eagles dotted the sky above. A similar mountain sunset finished off the tip of the rear fender. Then I drove the parts back over to Dennis's house to try my hand at clear coating.

After the paint was dry and all the parts new, used, and rechromed were collected and accounted for, I reassembled that knucklehead chopper and lit it up in the record time of five days! I was living the legend!

*Chapter Sixteen*

# Skid to a Stop

Victor DeBlasie worked in the Newark Police Department and lived at the lake several blocks from me. He was a skinny Italian guy of average height in his early thirties with thick straight black hair and the coolest handlebar mustache I had ever seen. Victor was married with two children and he was always laughing about something. He loved smoking pot and his humor was contagious. His policeman buddy Angelo was a big man that rode a Harley and dated a local girl. He helped Victor get a deal on a Harley that the Newark Police Motorcycle Unit was selling off. Their friend Dino who used to be a disc jockey for a small radio station and was putting himself through medical school rode a 750 Honda. Lastly Lenny, who now delivered potato chips, had invented some kind of soap product while living in Germany years ago and made a small fortune which disappeared as fast as it came to him. He took it in stride and was now looking to find a wrecked Honda 750 to build a custom from. I found him just the bike.

We often gathered at Victor's to smoke some pot, play a little guitar, (Victor had a beautiful cherry red Les Paul Junior) and laugh a lot. It felt safe there. No one was going to raid a uniform policeman's home.

Victor loved to make up names for everyone. Because of my painting skills he called me "Jimmy Dunes" and formerly "James Dufra Dubois" and then he'd laugh hysterically. For short I was "Dunes', and my girlfriend Liz was "Bones."

Victor's dream was for us guys to mount up and ride our motorcycles to Niagara Falls and on to Toronto Canada. He talked about it over the Christmas Holidays planning it out with Angelo and the other guys and began bugging me all spring to ride with them. I said no a lot and finally as July approached I just said "Call me in the morning the day you are leaving and if my duffle bag is packed and my bike starts up I go with you."

I asked Liz what she thought and she said it would be a good "guy thing" to do and something to remember my friends by. Victor and his wife Gail were also planning to move their family to Texas and open a sandwich deli. Lenny was going to go with them as well and our gang would be broken up for ever. Victor and Gail had been together since high school and what I did not know was that Victor and Gail were going to break up quietly out there because their time had passed and with Gail's knowledge he had been seeing a girl for over a year. Somehow they were all remaining friends. What else I didn't know was that Liz and Gail had been talking about the marriage breaking up and Liz was getting ready to move on as well. Of course the one being dumped is the last to know and that would be me. They all decided not say anything to me until the trip to Canada was over.

Seven thirty a.m. came with the garage phone ringing.

"Are you coming?" Victor asked excitedly.

"My bag is packed and my motor is running." I answered almost reluctantly.

At the garage Victor informed me that he had stuffed some joints into his handle bars and he and Angelo were carrying their Police IDs in case we get searched at the Canadian border.

The ride was slow going on my ridged framed bike and that pissed Angelo off who was in some kind of a hurry, but the rest of the guys were good with that and for relief Victor was begging to switch bikes with me for a while. He loved my chopper and wanted to be seen as a free hippie rebel at least for a moment. We switched back in an hour and when we reached the border I was the one who most fit the profile. Everyone's IDs were checked but of course my by bag alone had to be searched.

We stopped at the falls and then as evening approached we headed toward our camp sight to loosen up. The ride now would be a short scenic hop along the river so I broke my rule and undid the sweaty chinstrap to my helmet.

The road was one lane each way and we were typically riding two by two. Dino was in front followed by me with Lenny lagging on my right and Victor and Angelo side by side took up the rear position.

A fog rolled off the river and the pavement was sandy and damp. About two hundred yards up the road a sightseer slowed in the opposite lane and a second car rear-ended the first blocking off the oncoming traffic. The third driver in that lane responded by attempting to sweep around the collision causing the car in front of Dino to lock his brakes. He skid counterclockwise facing the crashed vehicles and the whole bunch blocked off both lanes. Dino had the presence to roll to the right shoulder and just escape the pile.

I press down on my rear brake pedal and catch Lenny skidding off to my right blocking any chance for escape in that direction so I push down harder on the brake and lock the rear tire briefly until my bike begins to pitch left and the rear wheel tries to catch up to the front on my right side. I let off of the brake quickly and the momentum snaps my ride upright but I'm still heading straight into the broadsided car. Again I press the pedal until she skids and pitches taking some of the energy out of roll but I 'm heading down for the tar unless I release. Once more off the brake and once more I'm up but the driver's side door is looking defiantly solid. It's time to choose the road or the car and amazingly I'm thinking of how I'll get home with a wrecked bike if I live! I know to keep my hands away from the ends of the grips to try to save them and I lift my left leg up knowing that the machine will spill over on that side, while I press the brake for the final time.

In an instant we're down and my metal monster screeches in anger enraged at the road. I blink with every bounce my body painfully takes.

The first sends my unlatched helmet into space. It is like watching a silent film. Each blink is another frame as the bike and I separate more and the car grows larger still. When I finally stop traveling my legs are almost under the rear quarter of the car and when I turn my head to the right the tip of my nose caresses the trailer hitch ball on the car's bumper.

The boys all made it safely and Victor and Angelo ran to help me from behind while Dino and Lenny returned from further up the road. They recovered my bike from the center of the road and put her up on the kickstand and began checking us both out. I had a large bruise on my left knee where it contacted the gas tank on my way over the bike, but beyond being banged up no bones were broken and no blood was gushing.

My Harley too had done fairly well. She had shaved off chrome from the foot rests scraping the road and the gas tank lost some paint where my knee hit it. Lastly when my wheels pointed strait my handlebars were heading to the right, but like we did when we were kids, and "I kid you not" I squeezed the front tire between my hurting legs and with my arms I muscled the bars back into place. The ring around my headlamp was scuffed but the light still worked on both high and low beams.

The next day we cruised along Lake Ontario to Toronto for a meal and then as the rain clouds gathered we started our long dangerous trek home. By the time we had crossed back into Pennsylvania It was night and raining hard. My chopper was a fair weather vehicle which had no front fender so if I hit a puddle my pant legs would get splashed. Riding on wet roads in the rain for anyone on a well-equipped motorcycle with fenders, crash bars, and hydraulic brakes on both wheels is dangerous for even the well skilled rider. My motorcycle had none of those features. Even my rear fender was narrow and short and water rooster tailed from it whenever the tire got wet. My rear wheel stopped with a mechanical drum brake which has much less stopping power than a hydraulic or "juice" brake and the feel or touch takes a lot of practice to get used to. In the years that followed, first automobiles and then motorcycles became equipped with hydraulic disc brakes which have the most stopping power and are least likely to lock up the wheel when applied. A driver of any kind of vehicle should know that when the wheels lock; skidding begins and steering control ceases.

This was essentially a 1946 Harley Davidson with much of the same engineering of that era. Harleys of that time had no rear suspension for shock absorption and often the rear tire would bounce on rough roads or unfriendly pavement.

The front fork on my motorcycle was an antiquated design as well having rods and springs without any hydraulic shock absorber to dampen chopping or bouncing of the front end should the road be unfavorable. Also I had the popular "spool wheel" for the front which looks lovely and graceful but offers no brake attached to the hub and the ultra narrow tire has a tiny footprint. That means that not a lot of rubber meets the road which translates into a bumpier ride sending shockwaves up into the handlebars and reducing control considerably. Think of it as a rolling ice skate.

In addition to three days of hard distance ridding, sleeping on the ground, recovering from having crashed, the darkness and the rain; a huge rooster tail of rain water was now constantly spraying exactly like a garden hose off of my uncovered front tire directly onto my exposed chin and neck.

My best scenario was to control the speed I was traveling to adjust the height and pressure of the spray and deal with all these afore mentioned conditions including the truck traffic which swamped everyone as well.

The night dragged. Our eyewear had no wipers. Neither your leather sleeve with zippers, nor your leather ridding gloves have any success clearing your distorted vision. If you remove the glasses the rain drops will now sting your eyes as well as your face at almost any speed of travel.

On the top of the globe that held my headlamp was a small red button light that remained lit when my high beam was in use. In the night rain with my soaked glasses the red light reflected off of the water and made a long narrow beam straight upward in my line of sight. My solution was to line up the red lazar-like beam with the appearing lines on the highway and as long as they were parallel I was in my lane riding upright.

Well you must know that giving enough time watching any line at night becomes quite hypnotic and eventually I blinked three times and actually passed out!

Any distance rider can tell you that after driving for hours (days) on end your muscles lock into position making any motion including steering very difficult and dismounting a real chore. Fortunately for me I did not instantly relax when passing out and for those short moments, I held the motorcycle fairly straight. A tractor-trailer had been behind gaining on me and because the throttle had a spring tension return, I began to slowly lose power and drift toward the shoulder of the roadway. When the truck driver blew his air horn my eyes popped open and I watched in horror the guard rail swiftly passing alongside my right leg.

The highway itself was paved with concrete sections that caused a bump every time you crossed a section, much like when a train crosses over the joining sections of rails.

The road shoulder was made of tar sloping slightly to the guard rail for drainage. Where the tar and the concrete slab seamed together, the tar dropped about an inch below the concrete being more elastic, so now I was riding on the sloping tar that was receiving all the wet runoff from the highway and washing it under the guard rail. Only forward momentum was keeping me from the rail and that too was decreasing at an alarming rate. My review mirrors were reflecting the blinding lights from the truck into my already impaired vision and I was calling on God for His favor.

Each time I maneuvered my thin front wheel to rub the edge of the concrete, the highway repelled my tire toward the guardrail. After two failing attempts to climb up the short waterfall I gave myself a small space, took a breath and then struck the back of my right handle grip with the palm of my hand and popped my wheel onto the concrete. Fortunately for me the rear tire followed behaving and now I was cautiously increasing the throttle careful not to spin the rear tire that was actually riding on a cushion of water and pull away from the looming front bumper of the tractor-trailer behind me.

Thanks be to God I made it through safely!

After the truck passed we all pulled to the shoulder and composed ourselves gratefully.

Having appreciated the dilemma Dino reminded us that he had *presided* over a college fraternity only a few years ago and that his picture remained on the dorm house wall of fame. The college dorm was about another half hour away and he was certain that we would be able to get hot showers and spend the night in the bunks. It was now after three o'clock in the morning and we all were soaked and road weary so we mounted back up and headed to the dormitory.

It was approaching four am and still raining hard when we pulled up to the dormitory with all its lights out. Dino rang the bell and banged on the door insisting that the place is never empty even during the summer break, but no one answered. Next he suggested that we all rev up our engines and awaken whoever may be asleep in the building. This delighted Victor who smiled, eyes popping, and encouraged us all happily. Again no one came to the door but Dino was not deterred.

"I'll find an open window and crawl through and come around and unlock the door!" He said smiling.

Dino disappeared inside and there was silence at first, then muffled bumping and crashing which continued for moments on end until Dino finally appeared opening the front door.

Smiling grander Dino explained that there was one guy and his girlfriend house sitting the dormitory while all the other students were gone and he found them hiding in a closet fearfully repeating, "Please don't hurt us!"

It seems that a week before we arrived there another group of bikers had come to the dormitory quite rowdy striking fear into the residents who after which decided they needed a break from the excitement and headed home leaving the young couple alone to stand guard.

Dino marched his reluctant captives to the hall of fame insisting that he was the former president of the dorm and finally persuaded them with his driver's license and matching portrait on the wall.

We had heavenly hot showers and cots to sleep on, a wonderful night's rest and best of all we had a tale to tell!

Liz and I had a wonderful and exciting three years together but that wasn't meant to be forever. Her parents were no fools and their girl was going to finish college. Rightly they were not interested in her hooking up with a long haired bearded biker like me. They never said it outright but I felt it everywhere. Liz wanted the American girl's dream; a house with a picket fence, three children and a husband with a regular job. I knew I had no means to give it to her and I wasn't ready for that road. She had gotten a job working with children at a Latchkey Daycare and loved it. She met a counselor named Carman and waited a while for me to save her. I couldn't. I knew it was best for her, but I didn't know how bad it was going to hurt me. It felt like I got my payback for leaving Joanne. For the next year that was hell on earth for my soul.

That fall Victor, his girlfriend, Gail his wife, and their friend Lenny moved to Texas, and so another chapter ended in my young adult life.

Jimmy Hawkins and I had been drifting apart since I went to college and we spoke less and less often. One day I was walking down Lake Shore Drive and I couldn't believe my eyes, I saw Jimmy Hawkins walking toward me carrying a pillow case full of his laundry with his head completely shaved. I didn't know if he joined a cult or what happened to him. As I began to walk with him to his parent's house to do his laundry he told that Mario caught him stealing stereo equipment from the shop and selling it off with another guy who I never cared for. Apparently Mario sat Jimmy down in the back of his store and shaved the thief's head as a shaming statement of guilt for the public to witness. I was left out of the loop because Mario was my friend and Jimmy got the job there because we were good friends. Jimmy kept his stealing silent from me knowing I would never approve and might rat him to Mario. Mario knew that I had no knowledge or part in it. Nevertheless my feelings were hurt that Jimmy could do such a thing. My feelings were hurt deeper because when we got to Jimmy's parent's house his step father came out and started yelling at me and accusing me of corrupting Jimmy! He told me to stay away from his son and his family. I lost my friend. I never saw Jimmy Hawkins again.

I remembered Sam De Croce and the nursery rhyme. I remembered my father and how he communicated honor, such a golden quality and so rarely seen. I remembered Jesus being accused and rejected.

By now my sphere of friends and influence had broadened giving me relationships up the hill into the higher, middle class neighborhoods. I hit it off well with Craig Davis. He was the youngest of three boys and about a year older than me. His father was an architect who had died when Craig was a boy. With long brown hair, blue eyes, and nicely muscled, he was a charmer. The girls flocked to him. He was bright and witty and spoke with an inviting soft tone. He played the guitar a little better than me and he drew and painted not as well as me. We both built Harley choppers with skill and we all smoked pot. Even Craig's mom, though she was carful not to let it get public. Mrs. Davis was a school teacher that wasn't trying to get in with a younger crowd.

No, she was just a liberal thinker.

Craig and I had another thing in common. We enjoyed shooting cocaine into our veins.

Ten years later Craig Davis would die from a heroine overdose in the bathroom of a fast food restaurant.

Malcolm Taylor, a heavyset black man the graduated high school with me, was now renting a room in the Davis home. "T" as we called him was not into hard drugs, though he would smoke a little bud with us. "T" had a tremendous sense of humor and exuded kindness like no one we had ever met. He was a gifted friend, a big cuddly bear, who encouraged me to continue with my artwork. Malcolm died a few years later at twenty four years old in a head on motorcycle wreck with an oncoming car.

Dave White lived in the Glacier Hills subdivision near the Davis family and he contracted me to paint his Sportster. I gave him a sunburst background under an ocean scape with a lovely translucent nude falling backward into the triple deep scene. Dave liked naked ladies and asked me to paint another smoking a joint hidden with two cherries on the frame where the front fork gooseneck meets the backbone and lower legs of the frame.

My sphere of influence was growing.

*Chapter Seventeen*

# MEET LOUIE

I had this tendency to collect different buddies like lost animals. I think because I always felt out on the perimeter of the popular crowd. In junior high Bob Korth and I gravitated to each other. Bob had a genius IQ and didn't relate to many people very well but we used to meet after school and play endless games of ping pong and began writing a science fiction comedy play that had us laughing hysterically for years. After high school Bob went on to Stevens Institute for a year. He was an agnostic scientist who became a believer in the resurrection of Jesus and then married his high school sweetheart making me his Best Man. That was awkward for me, but Bob really wasn't close to any other guys, and it was an honor to have his friendship and exchange dialogue with his brilliant mind.

Like that relationship, I had met in my travels another quiet friend who was cool about smoking weed and occasionally we would have laughs after his shift ended at a local filling station.

On one of those occasions we were discussing the quality, access and pricing of the said market and he said that he had a distant friend that would like to meet with me discreetly. When the friend of a friend of a friend trail ended I found myself six hours from nowhere sampling joints of reefer that were practically rolled in newspaper.

Louie was almost invisible in the room full of the smoke he exhaled with one release. He had a tremendous lung capacity. He asked me if I was a cop and passed me the joint that I was obligated to smoke while he explained the quality of that particular batch and compared it with two more reefer products on the wooden table, insisting that I sample each for science.

Another loner and a brilliant man that served no other purpose in civilization but to distribute hemp, Louie was the quintessential shadow person from a lost tribe of shadow people. Though he was not a shaman, he could shape change and disappear. Unlike the Chameleon that you can't forget or some exotic fish that dramatically mimic their surroundings, Louie was more of a blender. A blender became a term I used to describe the cars and trucks we used to transport our product. Statics revealed that in the auto industry the most popular color car was white followed by blue. White blue and grey finishes easily became lost on the freeways. For the purpose of blending into the traffic we would purchase and use the most average business coupes or sedans that looked like a million other such vehicles passing on the highways. Louie was like that. Even if I could describe him, that image would fade as fast as I spoke it, and smoking reefer enhanced the forgetting substantially. He was however courteous, well-spoken and powerful as well as a fair, honest and a very smart businessman. He was also paranoid. Louie changed meeting places constantly and moved his residence as often as twice a year. To the world as you know it he was nobody, he didn't exist. We had the same business philosophy and similar goals for retirement. Our partnership lasted about a decade.

*Chapter Eighteen*

# DARKNESS FALLING

My life consisted of building and painting motorcycles, painting murals on vans, and smoking and selling weed. I was "Weed Hopper." I had put that year in college, but couldn't deal with it though my grades were good. I was paranoid and distracted, and since my college girlfriend Liz moved on with Carman, my heartache endured. At first I got on my knees and pleaded with God to bring her back to me. That wasn't His answer. Then I chose to be foolish and beat myself up. To get God's sympathy or attention, or maybe to get Liz's I started shooting cocaine into my veins for the next year. I tried to go back to college, study art and humanities, but that wasn't going to well with coke addiction. Not surprised?

Wisely I turned to my God given gift for solace. I began to draw again.

## *Drawing Jeanine (as Debbie named her)*

I never had a complete faith in my art talent even though I had won those competitions growing up, but I hoped that it was something I could return to as a safe haven. I thanked God for the talent, and to comfort my bruised ego I began practicing by drawing beautiful girls from photos in magazines. My eyesight was superb then and I produced amazing detail in my drawings on manageable 8 ½ x 11 sheets of white typing paper and colored pencil drawings on colored chanson paper.

Of course my favorite source of reference material was *Playboy* magazine. After all, it was art! I searched for imaginative poses, sexy but not pornographic. I was on a journey to visualize my soul mate, that perfect beauty. I made several precise drawings until I felt my skill levels attain peak performance. With crisp pencil points and perfect pressure *Jeannine* began to look back at me with her distinct intelligent sensual warm captivating eyes. She sat watching me comfortably in a chair with one foot on the seat cushion, her elbow resting on that knee as her fingers slowly curled a lock of her long curly hair. Jeannine was waiting for me in an unbuttoned satin and lace negligee draped around her slender figure like open flower pedals.

For many years I considered this my finest drawing ever. It would test me more than a decade later. For the present it separated me from other guys. I alone had this unmatched gift.

Without a career, college or girlfriend in my life now, I needed direction. I wanted to belong. I felt isolated and lonely. As a man I wanted, to be worthy, to be affirmed. I wanted to be somebody. Selling pot gave me a certain control over my life. I served a purpose. I had an impeccable reputation for being honest and trustworthy, a rare quality that was universally sought after in the black market. Slowly I became legendary. There were some flies in the ointment though.

Over the years cocaine became the high society drug that attracted girls, but underneath the glamour lurked needles, and needles brought dopers and dope, that's heroin, and that's trouble.

I had made the best coke connection and my biker friends liked that. Joey Zip liked that. He liked that a bit too much. He shared some with a local junkie called Rothie. They jumped in Zip's Camaro and picked me up to make a deal. Rothie slipped into the back and I jumped in the shotgun seat. I had a heaping gram of pearly chunks that you could smell three feet away when the tin foil opened. Joey reached under his seat and swung a .357 revolver to my temple. "How about we just take it from you." he threatened. Joe was a real tough junkie. He had no problem offing anyone. He was real bright and hypnotically charming when he needed to be. He could talk his way out of a police station. But he was also vicious and ruthless, and an incredible schemer. If he didn't like you, you were as good as dead. If he liked you he was an incredible ally to have on your side. Right now he liked cocaine.

I stayed cool. The Jersey City Boys said that I was made of steel. "I suppose I could get nervous and spill this on the floor, and you could shoot me, but then at best all you'll get is what's on the floor, and you would've lost the best connection you ever had." I said calmly.

His eyes lit into a smile, "I like you!" he chuckled. I made sense, I was valuable to him. He became loyal to me. My life was spared and I had a new asset, Joey would do anything and I might need that someday. I already had a collector, Casey, the big tall biker who graduated from the Gulf station, was fast with his hands and wasn't the least bit afraid to fight anyone. He bounced in bars and schmoozed the chicks. I gave him wholesale prices on drugs as well as on painting his Harley and he looked out for me. We were close pals with a lot of mutual respect and loyalty. We had this in common, we both commanded power and we both had a reputation for it. If I needed something collected I could count on Casey getting the job done right. No repercussions. He had looks and brains to go with his skill and size, and he used his brains first to convince someone to choose to pay up. He backed his word up and never backed down. He always finished the job. He always won.

Now if someone was completely irrational, why waist the talent? I could let someone equally unreasonable deal with the problem; Joey. That was no problem for him either.

By now Casey was bouncing at a local tavern we called A-Dee's. Big Harold Clooney was tending bar there. They served shrimp and clams and huge roast beef sandwiches. When Casey and Harold were on the same night, "Anything goes!" Casey loved to dominate by show of power. He made condescending remarks to guys in front of their girls, just to boost his ego. Either subtly or blatantly he challenged everybody sooner or later.

He and I had a more sophisticated form of fencing. On my twenty fourth birthday he mixed me drinks, seeing if he could whittle me down with alcohol. He loved to see someone get screwed up, especially if he was responsible for it. I faired okay, but I left my car at the bar and walked home that night. It was only seven blocks. I got him back when it was my turn.

## *Hackettstown*

I bought a black 1975 Sportster with lots of extra chrome that winter. There was only 2800 miles on it.

At his request I painted a topless girl on a white horse on Casey's Sportster.

Smitty had an 86 cubic inch stroked Sportster that was way too powerful for a skinny kid on Quaaludes. Henry G. built racing motors and this number for Smitty was exceptional.

Michael Wrinkle was my friendly rival for air brush work, his work was better than Dirty Ed's. He painted Smitty's bike often because Smitty crashed it at least twice a year.

Joe Zip had a chopper Sportster that he just won a show with a week ago. Dirty Ed painted it and the mural was cartoon like compared to the art work I did. Casey laughed as I interpreted the lollipop trees, but it was good enough to win shows.

Dirty Ed rode a beefed up Honda 750, it was road ugly but it packed a punch.

We all decided to ride out to the Delaware Water Gap that Sunday from my place in the lake. It was a beautiful sight.

We lit the motors as the locals watched through a chain link fence at the beach across the street from my home. Generations of kids would grow up over the years that I lived there and built and painted motorcycles in that opened garage, and look on from the lake or wander up the driveway on their bicycles to check out the hippie bike builder's latest creation.

With the engines warmed we rolled down the driveway and headed the wrong way in single file down Lake Shore Drive as the cars and pedestrians parted courteously. Then pairing off two by two on Kingston road the open drag pipes that we all sported began breathing a little heavier as we motored up to the top of the hill.

Next the whole group leans to the right in unison into the loop the drops you off onto route 80 west. This is the launch. Here if you have any fear you'll fade away fast. Ramping onto route 80 here becomes a long time tradition. Casey and I were becoming legends. We hold our lower gears a little longer and pour more fuel on. Casey and I watch each other's face beam as we snap our shifters into the higher gears. The bikes surge forward together and the pipes thunder loudly. If you have a speedometer it is reading 100mph or more as Casey and I level our throttles and take casual poses in the saddle. We are laughing and signaling each other to look behind and see where the other guys are as we recalibrate our speed to 80 mph and let them tighten up the swarm. They got the message. For the next twenty miles we split lanes and take turns bursting through holes in the traffic and regroup for another burst. Yeah, its hell on wheels and easy rider all rolled up in one big present moment when Joe Zip slides up on my left side with his chopper show bike and indicates that he has a lifter tapping. Casey checks his mirror to see my head tilt right and he cuts the throttle and the group rolls into a trucker rest stop. We all kill our motors except for Joe, and the boys light up their smokes. Joe idles his motor next to me so I can hear the valves. I point at the rear intake and he shuts her down. Casey begins a barrage of hilarious quips and no one is safe from his wit except me. Our respect for each other goes way deep.

Intuitively Casey starts carefully removing Joe's spark plugs while Joe straddles his bike waiting for my command to slowly crank the kicker. I pop the clip and telescope the rear intake push rod cover and expose the rattling rod. I adjust the free play and check the other push rods while I'm at it. With the plugs replaced again we are ready to ride. Smitty and Joe Zip eyeball each other. Motorcycles and manifest testosterone takes over.

Smitty flattens himself forward over his fuel tank a dumps the clutch on his stroker right where the cam kicks in leaving tire smoke and sixty feet of rubber trailing behind as he reenters 80 west. Zip got the hint and kicks over his chop, drops his butt on the seat and dumps the clutch at a much higher rev. His front wheel bounces as he snakes a path into Smithy's smoke. Casey is laughing at my broad smile. We both know where Zip's lifters are going. Dirty Ed looks a little shell shocked but he is game for the ride, so the rest of us light up and follow the sound of blasting pipes. Smitty is probably in California by now if he hasn't hit anything. He has a habit of doing that. Fortunately he's had the good sense to release his throttle and look over his shoulder only to see Zip pouring it on. Something's up, I know. Again we all merge into the next rest stop about 100 yards before the bridge that crosses the Delaware River into Pennsylvania. Joe's gas tank has loosened up from the pounding and is about to launch off on its own.

"I got the wrenches." I state as I button down the loose parts, but this show bike is beginning to show some wear. The boys, on the other hand, are beginning to feel there oats.

Zip and Smitty are quick to light their motors. Casey and I exchange poker face glances. We both know well what is going to happen.

The stroker's 'R's are like the deep steady thunder of a diesel train on steroids, while Joe's chopper is screaming like a banshee. Yup, hell has come to breakfast.

Casey straddles his wheel with his long legs balancing as he lights a smoke with his Zippo. We both know that we're not going anywhere… yet. Dirty Ed always cautious, has learned to take his cues from us.

The stroker engine roars and Smitty dumps the clutch. Zip is quick to respond in like manner. Smitty's got two lengths on Zip as his tire hooks up, and Zip's front wheel is air borne heading toward the highway ramp. He winds up first gear to the max and bangs the forward control for second gear when parts explode off his bike and pinwheel like shrapnel barely missing Casey, Dirty ED and myself, driving into the cloud of smoke. The three of us have advanced only about fifty feet and easily bank right escaping the debris field. We shut down, drop kick stands, and run toward Zip who has bounced up on his feet and is already raising his bike back up. Joe is no daisy and can lift his bike like most people lift a lunch box. He doesn't have a scratch on him. It doesn't take a whole lot of time or effort to discover that Joey Zip has a charmed life. Although Joe is six feet tall with bulging biceps, he can disarm your sense of caution and invite you in his presence with a pair of magnificent twinkling blue eyes and a delightful smile that any politician would envy. Add to that his long blonde hair and soothing voice and many a lady will drop her defenses.

Quickly establishing that Joe is not hurt in the least, our attention turns to our next concern.

We help roll the tattered chopper off to the side while our street tuned survival instincts begin to engage. The New Jersey State Police patrol this stretch of highway and our fractured folly is just settling down.

Smitty is a mile away and will need lots of braking distance and a U-turn to find the condition of Joey and locate our pack, meanwhile the remaining four of us survey our situation. No one has stopped to help or investigate, and no sirens are heard. As far as the eye can see, no police are in sight. Smitty returns and confirms that the coast is clear. So for now Joe aligns his 'a little less than show bike' parallel to the grassy slope he is seated on and we assess the damage.

The cause for the damage is obvious to me. Traditionally, from the earliest years that the Harley Davidson Motor Company began making their overhead valve V-Twin engines with a separate transmission unit, the company has mounted the rear brake pedal on the right side of the motorcycle with the front brake lever mounted on the right side of the handle bars as well. Conversely the shift lever and clutch release are both actuated on the left side of these motorcycle.

On the other hand all Harley Davidson Sportsters built before 1975 have their rear brake pedal mounted on the left side of the bike while the foot shifter is mounted on the right side, a mirror image of the well-established norm for the big twins. This is further complicated by the mounting of the front brake lever on the right hand side and the clutch lever on the left, same as the Big V- Twin models do.

So it is that from Harley's roots to today's present Big V-Twin models, these motorcycles are operated by using your right hand and right foot for stopping the motorcycle, and using your left foot with your left hand to change gears. Again on the Sportsters built before 1975 the feet controls are opposite while the hand controls are still the same.

Confused? So was Joe Zip caught up in the moment, launching toward the rest stop exit in a mad dash to destroy the powerful stroker burning rubber between Smitty's legs. In his valiant attempt to get the edge, Joe took the "Rs" to seven grand in first and power shifted into second... with the wrong foot... smashing on the rear brake and exploding the brake plate as the shoes grabbed the drum, sending parts into the air and actually wrapping the brake actuating rod around the rear axle like a spool of thread!

When the roar, bang and boom ceased, and the smoke cleared, there was only left the smell of burnt metal, asbestos and rubber. I scoured for usable parts with Casey smiling on. Dirty Ed was dumbfounded.

Casey and Zip looking like an emergency medical crew, lifted the damaged bike to the side of the knoll since the rear wheel was jammed up with broken parts, and Zip, with my approval sat down on the knoll and began removing the log jam of parts sending them flying over either shoulder into the woods.

By the time Smitty returned from outer space, we had all the obstructing parts cleared off and the rear wheel could spin freely.

I suggested that one or two of us could ride to Joe's house, since it was nearest, and grab a pick-up truck, but Joe, being a seasoned biker said, "Nay, I can ride it home and just down shift to stop." Oh, did I tell you? This chopper had a spool front wheel to go with the extended

Springer front end. That simply means that there was no accommodation for a front brake. It would ruin the aesthetics.

I remembered having ridden my Knucklehead several times with no brakes as well so we agreed to the madness thinking that if he rides slowly near the shoulder and leaves plenty of space to down shift, a seasoned rider could arrive alive.

We mount up again and the five engines rumble to life. Joe Zip, true to form, screws his throttle wide open and dumps the clutch! His airborne bike shutters and leaps toward the highway. He's got the edge! Smitty, not to be out done, roars off in hot pursuit. Casey and I roll our eyes in unison and with Dirty Ed following behind, head sanely into the dusty trail.

We catch up to the crazies rolling off the last exit in New Jersey and we all loop around and rejoin the highway heading east toward Sparta where Joe lives. The motors wind back up and the wind hammers in our ears. I look down at my speedo and it hits a dollar and change (100+ mph) but I'm not catching up to Zip and Smitty. By the time I point at the rapidly approaching green exit sign for Hackettstown, Zip unloads his throttle and smashes his shifter into third gear. His engine screams in pain as he with Smitty glued to his tail, head into the exit. I'm squeezing down on both my brakes and the rest of the guys are doing the same. Zip's engine howls again in pain hitting second gear, and all of us are forcing our bikes to lean hard in the turn, Zip's high compression pistons are all the brakes he's got and if his motor pops from over revving, Zip becomes a skud missile.

But the truth is that Joe Zip is the world's greatest escape artist, ask anyone that survived a day with him. Heck, ask any cop or judge that's had the pleasure..! Zip makes Houdini look like an amateur!

"You can't make this stuff up! As the muses would have it, by the time our tires rolled onto Route 46, the summer humidity turned into a sun shower. Zip indicates that there is an open tavern just up the road where we get a bite and a beer and sit out the shower. We're all game. We strolled in like wet cowboys and surveyed the situation.

Casey and Zip were first through the door and if they didn't draw any fire or cause anyone to get too nervous, we would have no problems.

The bartender was amicable enough and there was only one young couple in the bar besides us. They were shooting pool while we hung our wet leathers on the backs of bar stools and ordered our drinks. Casey keeping his wits ordered a beer. I counted on him often to keep the peace. He never disappointed me. Zip and Eddy had the same. Smitty on the other hand had another game plan. It involved chewing a Quaalude and washing it down with 151 rum and coke as he starred out the open door from his stool with his saturated stroker in his direct line of sight. That wasn't good.

Not much of a beer drinker, I started my day with a screwdriver.

After two beers Dirty Eddy had an epiphany. "Let's play darts." Casey, true to form, perceived great humor in this and incited us all to have another round as the boys filed in line collecting darts. Now since the dart board was located beyond the pool table, it only made sense to us to throw the darts from our respective bar stools where we had continual access to our refreshments. But of course, all things being as they were, our aim was a bit off. Who knew? Casey knew as his twinkling eyes met my tight lipped reproof. Too late, the ball was in play, or should I say the darts.

Yeah, once in a while a dart did hit the board, but that was more the exception. Their flight path was precariously near the flesh of the guy and girl desperately trying to concentrate on playing pool and hoping we would vanish off the scene, when a stray missile struck into the border of the pool table inches from the hand of the crouching shooter covertly glancing toward the launch site. His eyes soon turned to the floor watching the approaching steps of Casey who kept the pool shooter in his sights as if to say, "Is there a problem?" Casey's huge right hand plucked the dart from the table and the dance hall player piano started up. Well, not really, but if there was one it would have. Actually the sound heard was Smitty's monotone proclamation, "Hey, the rain stopped."

Joe Zipp was delighted. We tipped the bartender and mounted up. Zip and Smitty sizzled on the wet pavement up to the traffic light. The rain came again. Zip, waving his arm and smiling shouted, "I know a better place on the way! We'll split a pizza."

This tavern was twice the size of the last and the place was hopping! Parked outside on trailers were race cars and drag bikes fresh from Island Dragway, the race track at nearby Great Meadows. The sunny morning kept the track open and the scattered sun showers pushed the excited motor heads into the local joints. We elbowed our way up to the bar and made room to sit together and have a pie. "You guys ride?" came a voice from the bar, "I had a bike once, it was a Triumph." Five pairs of eyes starred back silencing the voice. Casey was gracious this time relenting to verbally abuse the young man sitting nearby. It was the kind of bar where motor oil and gasoline vapors were scenting the grammar. And of course that only encouraged Smitty and Joe to have another showdown at the Okay Coral as soon as the sun returned. And it did. And they did.

Now you need to know that Route 46 is a local highway full of traffic lights and divided by only the double yellow lines down the middle. It is also noteworthy that this watering hole is on the west bound side, and we need to be heading east.

Smitty, fully loaded, lights up the stroker and burns another sixty feet of rubber in the east bound lane heading to the red traffic light. Zip, determined to catch Smitty at the light kicks over the once-show-bike and wastes no time circling east, but nails the hammer in an attempt to cross the double yellows and line up with Smitty. Horsepower and wet pavement compete for Joey's soul on the centerline of Route 46. If you never heard chrome scrapping pavement it is an unforgettable screeching as Zip goes down right in the middle of every moving thing. Eddy and I are dropping our kickstands back down and dismounting, while Casey has already leaped from his bike and is running to Zip blocking traffic with his presence in the eastbound lane. I'm running like a traffic cop with my hands stretched out in "stop" position across the westbound lane. We arrive seconds apart only to find Zip yanking his bike back up between his legs, and without checking a thing slams the kicker down, drops his but in the seat as he releases the clutch and is wheel standing his way toward Smitty when the light goes green! Smitty launches red hot on the green light and for a moment I forgot if it was day or night. You can feel the ground shaking through your boots. Casey and I, standing on the double yellows both agree that we last saw Zip's left forward foot peg dandling like a set of keys from the front of his frame. Zip has nowhere place his foot.

Well the sun returns brightly from behind the clouds and for the first time since this morning, our band of pilots roll slowly and cautiously into the very center of Hackettstown. I look up in disbelief at yet another red traffic light, and, like out of a Hollywood western I sense the strangest thing. It is probably 2:00 in the afternoon, but it might as well be high noon. Five engines are for the moment rumbling almost peacefully and not a human is in sight in the middle of town! Out of the corner of my eye I catch a woman hustling her son inside a building and closing the door behind them. No one is on the sidewalks and no cars are moving on the street. I take inventory of my boys. Casey is in front of me about three car lengths with Zip on his right, their long legs balancing their bikes effortlessly. Directly behind me I see Dirty Eddy in my review mirror. Deeply to his right is the ominous rumbling stroker motor of Bobby Smith, Sky Pilot. For the now all is cool and the motors are making a comfortable music in the bright afternoon light.

My eyes lift up to that red devil traffic light, and the thunder comes. My right ear drum begins to take the patter of a boxer's speed bag and both of my review mirrors are in for the same. I can feel Smitty's motor through my feet on the ground. I'm watching the light and my mirror as I silently count Smitty's r.p.ms. Two grand rolls up to three grand and holding, my mirrors are too distorted from the vibration to see with any clarity, so I look over my right shoulder to size up Smitty. He's got his head lowered to gas tank level and his eyes are poking out over the headlight. "Not good." I think.

But this becomes a three ring circus when my ears are brought forward to the pair side by side at the light in front of me. Casey is smiling big as he gooses his throttle up and down playfully inciting Mr. Zip. Joe takes the bait and responds with higher blasts. Casey works him like he has a monkey after a banana. Zip's motor responds with primal screeches, and then from behind the Stroker roars up to a steady four thousand r.p.ms.

I would swear I saw shades being pulled down when that demon red eye winked. You couldn't hear the five clutch levers release, but they all did. You couldn't hear anything anymore but the thunder. Wisely I throttled up and leaned hard to the left as a roaring chain saw stroker burning tar and rubber like a flame thrower raced by my right side. In front both Casey and Joey launched into wheel stands leaving smoke and fresh black scars on the pavement beneath them. Three bikes snapped into second gear under the green light. White tire smoke billowed out from Smitty's rear fender as he hit warp factor two. Eddy moved up to my right to watch the show when reality entered the next level.

At this moment you are five years old again, sitting on your living room floor watching the old black and white television while Dad reads the paper smoking his cigarette. Mom is in the kitchen with her bouffant hair-do happy as a clam making dinner. But you, you almost wet your pants when Rod Serling freeze frames the show and that tinny, ticking music starts while he speaks those familiar words, "It is a dimension of sight, of sound… the men you are looking at have just entered…" well , you know the rest.

"Twilight Zone" drops silently off my lips and time slows almost to a stall. The defining roar of many motors gives way to an eerie metallic crumbling crash.

Like a guided missile, Smitty's stroker slams into Casey's rear right shock absorber shearing it clean off Casey's bike. Out from the mixture of metal, madness and men, Smitty's Super SU carburetor and intake manifold bullet into a forward tumble like a stray round from a 45.

Joe Zip narrowly escapes the impact, but not for long. His front wheel touches down from his second gear burst, and as he is reveling in the idea of being lead dog, Joe turns his head to the left and back to find his friends, when he sees them in a tornado spinning right behind him. But it's too late for Joe's brain to process the info. Driving at high speed with no brakes and looking backward are never compatible, and Zip's handle bar clips off a mirror from a parked car that snuck up on him, and he grazes his boot along the door for balance. Now that clews him in as to how to stop his motorcycle, so Joey continues down the line of parked cars scraping them with his boot heel to create a little friction brake while grabbing for the occasional antenna to slow him down. It works rather well on the next three cars, but the line ends and Zip is still moving forward, albeit not upright. Without a car to buffer his travel his cycle finally bumps the curb, and, spilling on its right side, leaves Joe in a pile of parts and pills that dumped when the many baggies of ups and downs he stashed in every pocket split open.

Back in the Twilight Zone the early afternoon sun is smiling down on the center of Hackettstown. The explosive engines and the crushing squeals cease while the last plume of smoke and debris vanishes. All is silent now, too silent, except for the restrained voice of Casey explaining to Smitty how to separate their two bikes. No one is dead and no one is bleeding much. Except for a few scrapes and bruises the crew is intact. Eddy and I have parked on the right and as we walk to the first collision in the center of town, Eddy asks quietly, "Do you guys always drive like this?"

"That's how you get in the club." I reply.

"What club?"

"The Street Skinners."

"Street Skinners?"

"Yeah, you have to crash to become a member."

Eddy has no response for that, but my humor keeps Casey cool enough not to kill Smitty.

We got all the bikes to the side of the street and upon closer examination; at least Casey's was repairable on the spot. Smitty's front end ripped off Casey's rear passenger foot peg that secures the shock absorber to the swing arm, but the top fender strut mount remained in tact. All we had to do was relocate the shock back on the mount and twist a peg onto the remaining protruding threads. Other than that it took a few scrapes where the rest of the foot pegs and the ends of the hand grips ground along the pavement, his bike was more than ride able.

Casey walked up the street, retrieved Smitty's carburetor, and continued farther on up to check out Joe Zip's situation. Joey has his chopper back up on the kickstand, but the retracting spring that holds it in position is gone. In one day his show bike is nearly a basket case, and the day isn't over yet.

Our attention turns for the moment to the town around us. There is no traffic, no police no one entering or leaving the shops, just us, until we hear the muffled chatter of an old fifty's style farmer driven pick up slowly approaching.

"Howdy, you boys look like you could use some help." Offered the thin leather skinned smiling face.

We concluded that Smitty's Harley and Joey's ought to squeeze onto the pick-up, but Joe Zip assured us with confidence that his was drivable! Eddy was staring blankly while Casey and I rolled our eyes. We thanked the farmer and by the time we hoisted up Smitty's stroker, Hackettstown returned to normal life.

I blew my engine flying down route 287 North a month later. "Time to build another custom bike."

*Chapter Nineteen*

# THE WHITE SPORTSTER

I had a few paint jobs under my belt by now and my reputation as an airbrush artist at least locally was better than good. I had dirty Eddy and most of the other competition beat by a mile. Sonny Crone, and Chucky Jugens were well know master painters but they couldn't do the artwork I could. Les Dunnham was a big time customizer who created the Corvorado; a blended Corvette and Eldorado, among other nationally acclaimed originals at Dunham Coachworks, his lair in Boonton New Jersey. Les even admitted to me years later that he couldn't create airbrush paint like I could.

My favorite competitor was actually a guy one year younger than myself. Mike Wrinkle also didn't have what I have in artistic painting ability but what he did have he had plenty of. He shaped his projects into wonderful works of art. His body sculpting was superb and his painting skill was top shelf. Mike taught himself how to gold leaf and he was gold leafing gargoyles on his custom Sportster that year.

Mike and I were friends and we welcomed each other over with open arms to share knowledge and critique each other's work.

One year ago Mike was driving home from Atlantis City in his Caddy and fell asleep at the wheel. He hit the guard rail and split open the gas tank underneath the car as it hung on the rail leaning down on the passenger side where the fuel was draining. Mike couldn't open his driver side door and grabbing his shoes in hand had to exit through the flames out of the passenger door. Mike was pretty burned up and lost a couple of fingers from the fire but he kept both of his hands and legs and retrained himself completely and expertly without complaint even as his tender scarred hands moved in fiberglass resin and lacquer thinner while IV shunts were still tapped into the veins on the back of his hands. Mike was a living miracle and his work was flawlessly beautiful. I felt like I didn't deserve to compete with Mike Wrinkle, he was in a class all by himself. But we were custom bike builders and painters so we encouraged each other and went to work.

I took my blown engine out of the black Sportster and brought it to Henry Genoble with a sizable deposit. Henry was reputed to be consistently in the top three Harley performance engine builders in the United States. I explained my vision for the overall power and functional requirements I was going for and what I considered to be acceptable levels of maintenance and engine life as they relate to daily use. I conveyed my proposed artistic modifications in light of usefulness and flexibility in concord with aesthetic beauty. I was building a beautiful enjoyable Show and Street bike that could out perform the competition as well as excite the public and amaze the experts, converting the critics and convincing the judges.

Henry and I agreed on the particulars for my engine clutch and transmission, and the associated cost. At that time gasoline contained lead and you could purchase 101 octane at the pumps for pennies a gallon so using new high compression pistons was the hot set up. The stock compression ratio was around 9 to 1. My new motor would get 12 to 1 compression. A set of PB racing cams with solid roller lifters would add instant unfailing unlimited revs packing in the fuel mixture and blowing out the exhaust with longer duration and eliminating any chance of floating valves. The heads themselves were ported and polished to maximize flow. With zero restriction open chrome tuned drag pipes this engine was a real breather! That translated to instant useable horsepower. The lower end was perfectly balanced and blueprinted to exacting specs and the finishing touch would be the latest in carburetion, a Lectron Injector set up, but I was out of money now. *C and R Cycle* knew very well that I was the best airbrush painter on the east coast and offered to pay me generously if I would add my artwork to their painter's base color coats and win for them two coveted trophies: *Best Radical Custom Motorcycle in Show* and *Best Custom Paint in Show*, in the upcoming *New York Custom Motorcycle Show* held at the New York Coliseum in Manhattan.

I informed Ron Rebish the shop owner that I had only enough time to paint one bike for the show and, that I was painting and entering my own bike, and that my personal paint job would be unbeatable.

With that they offered to pay for all of my chrome plating including chrome plating my frame, polishing my engine/transmission cases and toss in the famed Lectron Injection system with a few bucks besides!

That sounded just about right, but I made clear one additional point. I would do their art work and it would win *Best Paint in Show* because it would be the best paint in that show; because my own bike would not be finished, and, no one could pay me enough to beat my own original creation. My concept was as unbeatable as my skills. I made it clear that after the *New York Custom Bike Show*, the most esteemed motorcycle show in the world, I would complete my motorcycle and paint job, and if our paths should cross at another show that year my own personal artwork would beat the job I did for them "No hard feelings". They agreed.

C and R delivered a diamond shaped, or often called a coffin shaped fuel tank, and a very basic five inch wide flat rear fender to me, both base coated in a blue-red flip flop dust pearl over black. In my opinion the painter made a mistake common to painters using the flip flop pearl dust mixtures. Whatever the reason, the paint manufacturer sends the premixed pearl highly concentrated. Perhaps the idea is to give the painter more bang for his buck. This paint thinned according to the label, looks like watered down milk in the gun, and the tint is almost invisible to the eye when the first one or two coats are laid out. By the time the pearl is noticeable the tiny dust of flakes are so built together that the undercoat has disappeared behind a gray shield, and the paint loses all its depth.

The only way to correct this is to start over with a fresh base coat of straight black and use my personal formula: Prepare a mix of your clear top coat. Vigorously stir up the factory pearl mixture labeled either *ready to use* or *thin 100%* and take one teaspoon from this and add it to two cups of the clear coat mixture. Lay on two even coats on each part and let it dry.

Now the pearl dust is properly separated and suspended over the black base making millions of tiny translucent stars that shift in color from electric blue to electric red embers and seemingly sink deeper and deeper into the black abyss.

It was too late to correct C and R's base coating. What they actually had now was a gun metal purple/grey haze as a base. "Can you work with that?" they hoped.

"Well you were going for a midnight sky idea, and I can still do something cool with that in mind. I'll shoot small clusters of stars here and there and add the moon with a frosty haze-like halo around it. I'll mix up your original pearls my own way to create an Aurora Borealis in the frosty night sky, darken in a horizon and paint a group of polar bears crossing the frozen waste on one side and a bald eagle here, a wolf howling at the frosty moon on this side and a Saber Tooth Tiger on an edgy peak with sparkling fangs on the fender's tail end"

They stared wide eyed with their mouths open in silence. "Cool!" they began to breathe.

C and R Cycle won *Best Radical Custom Motorcycle* and *Best Custom Paint* in the *New York Custom Bike Show that year.*

I completed my Sportster in pearl over white with nine interwoven murals that told a story as viewers circled the bike. You know they say "a picture says a thousand words" and this paint job had nine pictures interconnected. I had considered weaving as many as seven more into the whole but I stopped myself by thinking that this bike would be for riding as well as showing, and summer was approaching fast.

The "mind expanding" drug culture of the sixties lent itself to a lot of fantasy art on album covers and 'black light' posters. The opportunity was perfect for me to define my chosen reality in painting this bike.

Wizards were very popular but my core beliefs saw sorcery as a forbidden indulgence and I was not going to insult the True God and Creator of the Universe who gave this talent to me as a gift from a benevolent Father by glorifying His enemy with my use of it. No! I would do the exact opposite and make the work ultimately an homage to the True God! Even then worshipping God was not popular to express in our hedonistic society. This generation wanted no laws, only freedom to do whatever was natural or whatever was possible, yet I would remain grateful and faithful in my conviction regardless of popular beliefs.

I could compose in my head but I needed models for lighting and details so I collected all my resource and reference materials including a "Jesus Christ Superstar" album cover and a Moody Blues album cover, some Playboy magazines, picture books of other artists' work, and a copy of Kahlil Gibran's:" The Prophet". I even looked in the mirror for my own reflection.

With my collection of muses in front of me I began to spin my own love story of a man a girl and a horse trying to find each other and their Creator's plan while a darker power attempts to deceive, capture and destroy the dream as the onlookers all search the symbols and signs on the motorcycle's skin. In this story the good guys win!

I began taking trophies in the *Custom Street Sportster* class as well as *Best Custom paint* class. C and R cycle had the good sense to sell their show winner before I eventually went heads up with the new owner and did beat my *Best Paint* with my personal *Best Paint!*

## *Debbie*

One summer day I took a nostalgic motorcycle ride by an old friend's home. She was one of those girls you wish you could have as a real girlfriend but you became friends instead. That was never good for the ego but it did fill in gaps and young girls hang in groups which increases your exposure to new prospects. Darlene was a beautiful petite Italian girl with long black hair, lovely little features, and high cheek bones on angles an artist appreciates. And although I was her senior by two years, she shared the same birthday with me and cousin Marty. Truth be told, Darlene was gay.

With that I parked my show winning Sportster in front of Darlene's house and knocked on the door. Darlene's whole family was there, her parents, her younger brother Pat, and her older brother Ronnie who touted himself a genius with his bride Debbie. They were all Italian and Debbie spoke it naturally. She was a hair dresser having long thick wavy black locks, pale skin, bulging brown eyes and large breasts. And although I didn't find her attractive she was instantly drawn to "Jimmy Motorcycle" as I came to be known among them. And since Ronnie was socially disfunctionate, I appreciated having an alley that might bring leverage with Darlene. As it turned out Ronnie didn't smoke but Debbie and her girlfriends at the boutique were potheads and were more than pleased with my product. Selling them pot gave me a reason to be around and I always hoped to run into Darlene when visiting Ronnie and Debbie at their own apartment.

Unfortunately for us all the devil got in the details of my little plan to see Darlene. Debbie had fallen for me in a big way, initially hiding her true feelings in the form of friendship, and her friendship was soothing to me. She listened to my brokenness over love lost and wanted to heal me. Her husband the chemist was constantly proclaiming his intelligence and kept reminding Debbie that she was stupid. That alone can kill a romance.

Debbie saw my kindness as salvation and would tell her best friend

Tina that "Jima" as she called me "was so goddish."

When I planned to leave town for a week Debbie planned to leave Ronnie without my knowledge. When I returned she had her own apartment above Hal's Kitchen in Parsippany. I explained to Debbie that she was not the one for me though I cared for her and that someday I would find my own true love and she would have to know that I would be gone. She accepted this and after awhile got together with the guy I first smoked pot with. We three remained friends.

In a few short years Debbie died of a brain aneurism. She was twenty four.

## *The plague @ A Dees*

The 1970's rolled in on a disco ball with platform shoes. I wasn't made for this decade. Guys wore leisure suits while the "foxes' wore glam with big hair. The night life was line dancing, cocktails and cocaine. Then the movie "the God Father" made a way for us dealers to fit right in. Having money was cool again and eventually the men's clothes classed up nicely. I lost the long hair and beard and now sported a nice tight combed back haircut with a trim moustache.

Thankfully the platform shoes gave way to soft Italian leather and in the cooler weather we finished it all off with an expensive full length cashmere overcoat and a fine scarf.

I liked the look. I liked the overcoat. It had deep pockets inside and out. At that stage of the game I kept as much as a half-pound of pot in one ounce bundles on me inside the clubs without anyone blinking an eye.

This little Jersey town had five taverns within three miles of each other. There were two gin mills on the lake not two hundred yards apart. Jimmy's tavern was the bottom line. It had a real wood shuffle board table complete with sawdust, and you could get a glass of beer for twenty five cents. The low life cliental met there. Within eyeshot was the "Y-Knot Stop" formerly known as "Whitee's." It carried almost the same appeal. At least this place had a floor. They tried to class it up with a couple of scary tattooed go-go girls and even washed the glasses but as a landmark it gave the town no pride.

The third stop on Lake Shore Drive was Leo's. It finally changed hands, got a face lift and was renamed. Breze's was a safe half mile away and even couples patronized the place.

In another half mile tucked in with small businesses and apartments on a major road into town lay Ingrid's Rendezvous with a business lunch and conservative crowd.

Tucked off another road into town almost hidden from view we had the "Admiral's Daughter." The "A-Dees" was the place to be. Once a fisherman's bar, the Admiral's Daughter became the local nightclub for our generation. Big Harold Newman tended bar with my friend Casey who also bounced there all weekend. Some of the larger sized local law enforcement stopped in when they were off duty and made their corner of the bar look top heavy. They were cool and we had a silent understanding. If anything had to be said it could go through Harold who was their pier and our friend, or through Casey who everyone respected.

Bars were a natural playground for Casey. He was an unchallenged chick magnet. He had the mojo. Any charm the rest of us males might have had was diminished in his presence.

In those days everyone drank in the bar and smoked weed out on the porch in the dark, or in their cars and came back in for the music and to socialize with the young ladies. I passed off several ounces of pot on weekend nights there undercover and without incident until I decided not to sell those quantities. I had grown beyond that level eventually and I didn't want to take public risks being seen or be labeled a street dealer. I didn't want to make more acquaintances on that level. People with little to lose are by nature less cautious. Although some young dealers liked the title, it made them feel cool, like they were a modern gangster, I was not looking for the exposure. My goal was to make a little money and find a small business like a book store to operate and leave the black market. Smoking the stuff was getting scary enough and though it was exciting, the business was dangerous.

By 1975 a large number of people from all walks of life were not only snorting cocaine up their noses, but injecting it intravenously, people that you would never guess would do so, did so, like it was nothing. No longer was it associated with being a junkie, but being fashionably elite. That couldn't last. Christmas was coming soon and the weather was cold. The locals got of some good flake and some used needles and that set the town on fire. Contagious Hepatitis broke out to the level of the town giving free gamma globulin shots. Too many of the carriers had been patronizing the A Dees which sold shellfish and someone or something had to take the fall.

Because it was the type that is easily transmitted in ways other than intravenously, bad clams looked like the culprit. That killed the business for the owners and although the town's volunteer firehouse was right behind the Admiral's Daughter, it mysteriously caught fire about 4 a.m. New Year's Day and burnt to the ground marking the end of another era for our hometown.

*Chapter Twenty*

# ROXANNE

When I met Roxanne I gave up the needle, telling my buddy Anthony, "I'm not going to screw up this relationship by shooting dope." Of course I opted to snort it instead.

I was twenty four and she was thirty. Roxanne was going through her divorce. Her x-husband was living with his latest girl friend out in Illinois. He had a master's degree in something and a black belt in something else, and was teaching PE at a college out there. She was dating her boss Joe, who owned two restaurant/bars and a construction company. Joe gave her nice things, two beautiful diamond necklaces, and her choice use of either the red Eldorado or the TR3 convertible, along with some furniture etc. She had the sexiest sounding mellow voice. She liked the things I talked about. She liked my mind.

We dated maybe two or three times and she invited me over one day. Her X drove across the country apparently with the idea that he was going to kill someone. He broke in through the basement and made his way up the stairs to the living level. Roxanne grabbed the phone to call the police but he tore it from her hand, beat her on the back of her head with the receiver, turned and attacked me. His first kick broke my nose. The next shot snapped my jaw. The bone came right through my tongue. My last molar broke in half. The next time I awoke I was being kicked in the head with a tan construction boot. I felt like I was way under water and I heard him say twice, "He's dead... he's dead." My focus was dreamlike as I watched the boots disappear through the kitchen door.

I remember moving slowly so no body parts would puncture through my skin or just fall off. I rose with equal caution and observed the room. The walls the ceiling and the lampshade all looked as if someone had soaked a mop in a bucket of blood and splattered it everywhere. I walked cautiously toward the bathroom. From the hall I could see the kitchen doorknob Blood, my blood was everywhere. I turned into the bathroom and raised my eyes to the mirror over the sink. I never saw that person before. Frankenstein was peering back at me with a head the size of a basketball through bright red lines where the whites of my eyes once were. My nose was broken and bulging and dripping with blood, as was my lower lip. My lower jaw bone was broken through my gum and holding up the roof of my mouth which kept filling up with blood. Carefully I dipped my chin to let the mouthful of blood pour into the sink. Then I heard my name spoken quietly and in question form "Jimmy?" The EMT standing right in front of me was a guy I knew for twenty plus years. He wasn't sure who he was looking at.

Her X got a top shelf lawyer and did a great acting job for the grand jury. He got off. I had the option to sue, but she had two kids and I sold marijuana. We didn't need more trouble. Yeah, I had offers from dangerous people to "pay back," but that too was evil. I figured it best to take the hit. Perhaps God in His mercy would have mercy on me when I really needed it.

I paid out of my own pocket to have my jaw set and my teeth fixed. At 500 dollars a month it was a lot of money in 1977. I slept with a shotgun and raised Doberman Pinchers after that.

I suffered memory loss from the concussions, and had severe attacks that threw me to the ground with agonizing chest pains. For the most part they stopped after about a year, but a deep trauma etched in both mind and body relentlessly manifested in demonic fears decade after decade.

Roxanne and I stayed together but any chance for romance was destroyed. We just needed and helped each other. Roxanne did love me, but in a very possessive way. Kyrie Tatiana loved me in a very possessive way also and I was good with that. She was my Doberman Pinscher. I bought her at eight weeks old after meeting the dame who was aggressive, high strung and scary. I brought this black and tan pup home and kept her at my side always. She instinctively knew what to do.

In the spring of 1977 I had no money for paint. Roxanne lent me five hundred dollars for a pound of Colombian Gold. I sold it in ounces and realized a fair profit. I reinvested in another mix. It worked as well for me. I did it again and again. In a year the original five hundred dollar investment made me $35,000.

*Chapter Twenty-One*

# DOUBLE CROSSED TWICE

I bought my first Corvette for $1800. We had it for four days. Roxanne and I were having some stress so I suggested that we take the Corvette for a ride to Stokes State Forrest for a little escape. When we got to the woods I gave her the wheel to share the pleasure of driving the sports car on the back roads with the top down. We passed the old graveyard leaving the ravine and turned toward the one lane bridge made of wooden planks supported in an iron trestle. Our approach was a little too fast and the front right tire rode up the trestle like a ramp. We came to rest balancing the car on the bridge's iron work teetering slowly left to right with the nose pointing up in the air at a 45 degree angle.

I watched the folding headlight box spin down into the water below along with the directional lamp. Roxanne was stunned behind the wheel waiting for hell to break loose from my mouth, but I had the presence of mind to tell her gently not to move too suddenly and slowly release the brake with the clutch disengaged, hold the wheel still and see if the car would begin to roll backward and not off the right side of the bridge.

The Corvette was stuck upended and Roxanne was scared so I explained that if she got out before me the car might tip to the right and plunge off the bridge, but if I climbed over to the driver side before she exited entirely we just might keep the left front tire on the bridge. That plan worked and once I saw Roxanne walk clear from the bridge I started the engine and carefully put power to the rear wheels and dragged the nose of the car off of the bridge.

The right front bumper had bent back into the tire but not enough to cause a flat so I looped the cable guard rail over the bumper and again with the car in reverse I used the engine power to pull the bumper back out. That worked as well and since the wheel alignment wasn't too bad, I decided to hike down to the water and retrieve my parts and attempt the drive back home.

In the end the insurance company paid $4,600 for the Corvette to which I added another $600 and gave the money to Roxanne as a down payment on a house that would be purchased in her name only so she wouldn't be tied to me or my business should something go wrong, and if I died the deed would be solely hers unencumbered. It was a good idea and since the purchasing price was only $37,500 the payments would be a reasonable $350 per month. I let Rox handle that while I paid for a new roof and gutters, had the dirt driveway graveled and paved and had new carpet installed throughout the first floor. Along with remodeling the only bathroom and some carpentry work in the basement I installed a good used washer and dryer.

I had the help of a couple of friends move our furniture into the living quarters but no one but Anthony entered the basement which had existing shelves and a workbench in a far corner that I closed in with a dividing wall after we got settled. I blacked out the basement windows there and hid my scales among the now cluttered shelves. Alone I used the workroom for weighing and repackaging my product.

I had broken the cardinal rule.

Anthony was my best friend; we commiserated over our emotional garbage and shot cocaine together for a year. When you trust your life in someone's hands like that you become close comrades. I used to give a pound of pot up front to him at the wholesale price which I sold lots of twenties for. He got spoiled using the free credit I extended to him and never paid cash first.

This business was based on trust, its members survived because of their trustworthiness, or perished for lack of it. What I forgot was that each member had to have something valuable to lose for it to work. This one time my judgment was clouded by my faith in my friend and it was going to cost me.

Supplies of reefer came in waves because it was a harvested plant. This was good for business because it created scarcity. That drove the price up. For safety no one got the privileged information of knowing when the next supply would come to market until their own personal deal was in place. Wholesale dealers hoped to be long gone underground by the time the street had pot to smoke or sell.

All my men knew not to just drop by. I kept traffic to a minimum, social or otherwise, to avoid visibility to the law or to anyone that might notice a pattern. Even a casual daytime meeting could appear suspicious. Patterns are traceable and can be analyzed. Only those esteemed trustworthy on the highest level could attain the honor or assume right to visit. That right of passage usually came by having your character proven. Rarely was it ever granted. *Never* was the rule.

Anthony stopped by at the new place to see if I had any news. "Follow me." I said and led him down stairs into the basement and right into my workroom. "I got two small bundles," pointing to the plastic garbage bags on the floor "one commercial and one gold; primo. I got to move some things around today."

"When?" Anthony asked.

"Right now. You feel like taking a ride?" I spoke casually without revealing any emotion. I was an expert at it.

"Sure. I'm with you." He said softly.

I pushed one bag back under the workbench and grabbed the remaining bag.

"Which is this?" Anthony asked.

"The gold." I answered.

"The gold?" he asked again for conformation.

"Yeah, the gold." I said as I lifted up the bag and guided Anthony back up the stairs.

I tossed the bag into the trunk of the car and we drove down to my mother's house and backed up to her garage door. It was daytime and the streets were empty as I studied the perimeter. I opened the garage door half way and we scooted under with the bag and pulled down the door.

The garage was my motorcycle work shop and it was crowded with bike parts, in boxes, on shelves, and leaning against the walls. Lots of custom paints and tools filled the area as well. To the left was a wooden door that opened to the crawl space under the house that was used for storage also.

I pointed to the crawl space.

"That looks like a pain in the ass." said Anthony.

"Where?" I asked "Way back there?" pointing to the far wall full of stuff.

"Yeah that's plenty good. No one will look there." He said.

I walked the bag to the back and placed it under a shelf in the left corner and laid some things over the bag to camouflage it more. It disappeared.

"It's the gold right? 'cause I'm gonna want to get some." He asked again.

"Yeah." I said and we left. As I planned, it was almost three in the afternoon now and school kids and moms would be around soon, and the cops would circle the lake on patrol. There was an old dog in the house that barked when he heard someone approach. In an hour and a half my mom would be home from work and even she wouldn't know that I had been there. Mom was a deterrent by being home, and if the dog barked she would call the cops out of fear. A thief would have all those obstacles in his way if he knew I had just stashed something there. But of course only two people knew that right?

I never left my stash unguarded so why did I even make that move?

I got a phone call from the Jersey City boss the day before asking to meet casually for lunch. I knew by his tone the man had something important to say, so we met face to face and took a drive out of town where we wouldn't be noticed together and no ears could overhear our conversation. I had a lot of respect for this guy. He was all business and he backed it up. No one crossed him and lived to tell about it. His ship was tighter than a frog's butt and his men were real pros. We worked together on occasion and he had a big respect for me and let me know it. If he didn't I would have been out of play by now, either in jail or dead. These guys didn't like competition and didn't tolerate slip ups or loose lips. But I was an asset to him, like having someone watching your back door; we were there for each other.

"Jimbo, you working?" he asked.

"I got a little thing going" I replied.

"I know. I know" he stated and it was no joke. He had something serious to say.

"You got a close friend named Anthony?"

"Yes." I confirmed.

"Actually there are two Anthonys. One you may or may not know." he paused, "I'm going to tell you something I don't have to tell you." His lips drew tight "He set you up. You are going to be robbed. He knows the layout of your house. In your basement you have a workroom with a workbench against the wall. You keep your stuff there."

The dark specter speaking had never been in my new place. Only Anthony had been privy to my set up and he had a friend from his school days also named Anthony. That second Anthony was now a heroin junkie hanging with the lowest local junkies. My friend Anthony never mentioned him, ever.

"Remember, I didn't have to tell you this. I'm doing you a favor. I'm telling you before it happens. Don't ask me anything more about it. I am telling you what I know. Your friend is no good. He sold you out." Then the boss dropped me off.

I had plenty to think about. Could the boss be setting my friend

Anthony up? Maybe he knows how well I treat him and he thinks Anthony is a bigger player and wants to drive a wedge between us? But why go through the trouble, we all have too much drama already.

Maybe he wants to quench my independence from him and offer me protection for loyalty. And maybe he is a friend doing me a favor. That can only make us tighter. Usually the simple answer is the correct one, and the facts are staring me right in the eyes. He got the information right. It was undeniable, I just didn't want to believe it.

So I put it to the test, and like clockwork, the next day Anthony just happens by. I never open the bags in front of Anthony and he has to take my word that the one we move to the garage is the gold. Fortunately I lightened the bag to ten pounds, but that still cost me $3,500. I could have used a decoy bag but I was still concerned which location would get hit and I didn't want all my eggs in one place. I didn't have much time and I figured that I was being watched already by the bad guys. I'd prefer that they didn't come to Roxanne's house because that would mean a gun fight. They would have to kill my Dobermans and face my shotgun. That would mean "game over" for all of us: newspapers, jail time, dead people and Roxie caught in the middle could lose her house, joint custody of her kids (who were living with their father) and even her life if she showed up at the wrong time. No it was better to bate the thief to go where no one would get hurt. Junkies don't want jail time because they will go through withdrawl. They want it to be as easy as possible. If they only break in the garage and steal your pot who is going to call the cops to investigate a B and E?

After Anthony dropped me off I loaded my shotgun and rang my mother's house to be certain that she had gone to work. She did. I couldn't be in two places at once and the only guy I could trust to be over there was Casey and he had an honest job and two kids to raise and support. Anyway there was no time.

When Mom came home from work she called saying that the garage door window was broken. "Should I call the cops?"

"No wait 'till I get there." I said and headed over. The weed was gone, nothing else was disturbed. If it wasn't Anthony's accomplice it had to be someone with better than an eagle's eyesight. We had blocked the door unloading and never opened it wide. Also I pulled it down before stashing the weed and, nothing else was disturbed. There was no mess searching for the stash.

I told Mom that nothing was missing and that she could call the cops but they wouldn't do anything. "I'll put an alarm system on the house and the garage tomorrow." I said and called Jimmy D who worked in an electronics store that handled that stuff.

We put in a new window and then on all the windows and doors around the first floor of the house we added electronic tape connecting to a box in the closet and a fire alarm on the roof.

Now I had Anthony to deal with as well as the lost reefer and the rest of my dealers, and paying off my partner for the shipment. Plus if I don't fix this powerfully, the word on the street could be that I was weak.

I was supposed to be a man now and weigh out my own decisions. My father was gone over a decade and I was left to write the rule book so I used to pretend I could talk with him and get some superior wisdom.

"Whatever you do you will have to live with it and the consequences for the rest of your life." echoed in my head.

I called Casey. "I got a problem."

"Yeah." his voice sounded like the lowest note on a piano. "I'm coming."

We met at the garage and I laid out the whole story to him. I never told another soul.

"What do you want do?" Casey asked.

"I want to be sure. I don't want to hurt the wrong guy." Hurting people wasn't my style. It never restored things, but it did teach valuable lessons. "He lives with his parents and family. Let's go get him at home. We'll leave our car a block away and walk up to the house and knock on the door. I tell him we ran out of gas down the block and ask for a ride to the gas station. You get in the front and I'll climb behind him. When we get a block away I'll tell him what I know. You pressure him for the truth."

Casey's eyes were firing up, he was good at this and the corners of his lips raised at the thought of two micks taking a guy for a ride in his own car. That would be classic. And that's what we did. I wasn't going to let Casey bust Tony up, though he wanted to. My goal was to get the truth as painlessly as possible.

I sat in back and told Anthony that I got robbed. He acted surprised, but we could see he was guilty. I told him a little bird told me that His old buddy Tony and the junkies put him up to it. He swore he had nothing to do with it. Casey smacked him in the face twice and told him to cough up the truth. Anthony began to wail insisting he could never do that to me that I was his best friend, how could I believe that. Casey badgered him and he kept crying "I could never do that to you."

"I'm giving you a chance to come clean. It's not about the money. You could have had anything. Just tell me the truth." I said but he kept shaking his head and crying "I could never do that to you."

We made him take us to our car and we got out. Anthony rolled away slowly.

"What do you think?" Casey asked. I could see I didn't let him finish his work on Anthony but we both knew what that was about.

"I don't know" I shook my head "Who else could it be? The evidence given me before the rip was perfect and my source was solid. I just don't want to believe he did it."

"Yeah, I know."

A week later I got a hand written letter from Anthony saying the same stuff and how he understood that "in the business you are in you have to be tough." He had not seen tough from me really and I think he knew it from the beginning that I wouldn't hurt him. I think he counted on it. But I wasn't done looking for answers so alone I went back to the source of information. In the early morning I took a ride to the city alone, to the Boss's home. You don't go there without an appointment, but I went.

The caliber of the home was on par for the neighborhood so that it blended well. The service entrance was familiar for family and friends and would be proper protocol. I took the liberty to enter there. I was warmly greeted by family and invited to sit at the kitchen table while a member checked to see if the boss would receive me.

I was informed that he had just showered and I was invited to engage him as he shaved. This was a dangerous undertaking to the third degree on my part.

"Jimbo! How are you doing?" He was warm. That was good. "What can I do for you?" the Boss inquired as he headed into the bath and wetting his face with a hot towel and reaching for the lather.

I paused slightly to time this right but not enough to create any drama that might turn the ambience into suspicion. "Can we talk?" I asked permission.

"Sure, what's up?" he answered as he applied the shaving cream.

"You know they got me." I said as the razor touched his sideburn.

"Yeah," He gently stroked looking in the mirror, "I told you."

"Yes I appreciate it." I said watching him stroke his cheek. I needed a few more seconds for the razor to change direction.

"I took Anthony for a ride." I added as he stroked the opposite cheek in a downward direction.

"Yeah?"

Then the boss lifted his chin and put his razor to his neck and slowly began an upward stroke.

"Rothie got it." I said as the razor reached the corner of his jaw and stopped. Red blood began to invade the white foam. I knew then where my weed went and how the boss got his information. His eyes widened with fire, his face tightened and flushed while his chest filled with air. The Boss turned and starred me in the eyes while he pointed the razor like a knife at me, "I told you! I didn't have to tell you anything! That cousin of mine should be dead! Someone is going to kill the piece of crap!" What are you going to do? What do you want to do? I should've killed him myself! That scum!"

"Well this sucks" I'm thinking. "But I'm not dead yet. He is not beating me to death. That's good." My thoughts continued.

We both took a deep breath and composed ourselves. We were solid together. I was still golden to the boss. I took another slow breath and he did the same.

"Revenge is best served on a cold platter Jimbo." Boss stated.

"We good?" I inquired.

"The best Jimbo. You're the best"

"I can live with that." I thought.

While I left Anthony and his bruised ego on ice he turned to coke dealing. With *Tony Montana* his name's sake from the movie *Scarface*, as his mentor, he toughened himself up. In time I allowed him back into my good graces and tossed him a pound each time he came by to keep him busy where I could see him. Better a poor friend than a bitter enemy. Truthfully, I loved the guy.

I had a lot to make up for and no time to loose. The days blurred into years of lonely partying on drugs and alcohol and sobering up for the job. It was like watching a James Bond movie on bad acid. Roxie and I had no real relationship. We were never in the bed at the same time and when we were no one initiated anything. I think we both got tired of waiting. I don't know what we were doing together as a man and woman, but as soldiers we were both committed to holding the fort, and we were good at it.

One night even our fort came under attack. It was a Friday night, actually well past twelve and ironically both Roxanne and I were in bed beginning to dose off when we heard a car pull up crunching the gravel stones in our driveway. I had parked Roxie's inconspicuous little Ford Capri only half way up the drive way to cause any unexpected visitor pulling in to have his tail jutting into the street. What I alone knew was that there was a forty pound bail stuffed tightly into the car's trunk. Sometimes it is better to leave things where they are than to risk being seen carrying packages in and out of the house.

I peeked out of the bedroom window and saw the headlights shinning on the back of the Capri go out, but the invading vehicle was still running with two men in the front seat and no one was moving. Plus I didn't recognize this car. A friend doesn't show up unannounced past midnight unless they are in real distress, and even then if you were my friend you'd know better. I pulled the shotgun out of the closet and pumped a shell into the chamber. Roxie was heading for the front door intending to light the porch but I stopped her. Kyrie our Doberman was standing right at her side with her hair bristled, her body tense at attention. Should I walk out with the shotgun, or just point it out? Better yet, this house is only in Roxie's name, as far as the police know I'm not there. I can leave them the job of investigating this occurrence, and I won't have to explain what I'm doing brandishing a shotgun. The house doesn't get searched and Roxanne is an innocent neighbor, plus no one gets shot.

"Rox, call the cops and tell them an unknown car is idling in your driveway with its light off and two men are in it and you don't know who it is.

Roxie makes the call, Kyrie is barking fiercely and there is no movement outside. In minutes a police cruiser arrives blocking the car in the driveway from behind. Their spot light shines brightly on the unknown car and the trunk of the Capri as well. An officer exits each door of the cruiser and removes the men from the blocked in car. Through a window we could see that one was Carl, a guy I had met through some local bikers. The men are told to place their hands on the trunk of the Capri and are patted down and handcuffed. A search reveals a .38 calibur pistol and several rounds of ammunition lying on the floor of the car. The policemen call a tow truck to impound the car and then leave with their two suspects never knowing what was in the trunk of our Capri or who was in the house.

Roxie called the police station the next day and was informed that the two men had the gun and ammo and that they had been arrested a month ago for disposing of a corpse.

When it came to court Carl and his partner tried to say that they knew me and that they had known the house and could draw a picture of the basement attempting to infer that if they were pressed they had something to roll over to the judge, but His Honor refused to hear this portion of their testimony declaring that it was inadmissible and not related to the arrest and trial at hand. I had escaped exposure, and now it was time to weed out the bad apples. Without contact we silently agreed to bury this and they would respect my turf.

On two different occasions using two different cars each lost a water pump crossing a state line while transporting a load and both times I made it back undetected. One time I lost the pump in the Lincoln Tunnel. The engine got so hot that the pistons began to ping and rattle but I made it into Jersey and pulled into a gas station. When the engine cooled down a bit I added water and drove with the radiator cap loosened. I did a lot of praying on my job especially making these runs. You may think what you will, but I believe God had given me much mercy.

One night while high on coke in another state, I lost control of a car rounding a mountain curve in the snow and slammed into the rock wall avoiding the guardrail side that protected the cliff. The sedan bent at the roofline behind the driver and passenger doors but I continued on my mission.

Twice I had fuel lines freeze and had to get towed to gas stations where the lines thawed out. God had to be watching out for me.

In November of 1981 I felt obligated to help out Jersey City Boss to keep good faith. He had some really dry pressed bails that were tossed back in his lap. They smoked badly and somebody had added water to try to refresh them, but when they began to dry a second time they lost potency and weight. But there was a marijuana drought and the market was hungry as well as our pocket books. I was pressured to take them, and I did. Now it became my problem. I gave the package to Jimmy D on the cuff with the understanding that they would loose more weight if they dried again. He promised to keep straight with me and let me know if things were going badly. I assumed he had problems with the product, but worse than that, he got tied up in cocaine dealing with my old pal Anthony. If that pot made Jimmy any money, it went up his nose.

I asked Anthony to hold back on Jimmy D so I could reason with him and make a plan for him to work the debt off. Anthony refused me saying, "Business is business." I could have cut Anthony off again from getting my reefer in retaliation, but I wouldn't. I already knew his character. I just continued to believe that mercy reaps mercy and I had been getting plenty. I decided that it was better to keep him where I could see him than to create two new loose cannons that would need to be quickly taken out of play. It wasn't worth those consequences. Plus I'm still making pocket change on one of them and they both know I know bad people.

So for fifteen hundred bucks Jimmy D lost his opportunity to ever work with me again and I learned the same lesson once more on trust and loyalty, having a backbone of integrity and the tragic flaw of a warm heart. I also knew how valuable I was to the men on top. We were so few. You always have to weed out the garden.

As Christmas of 1981 passed, I was pretty much broke. I had for sale signs on most everything I owned.

I stopped to see Jimmy D. He had a new carved coffee table sitting on a new oriental rug and new his and hers skies leaning against the wall, yet he said he had no money for me, but if I had any work (pot) for him to let him know. That of course would never happen.

1982 rolled in like a Tsunami. Louie's connection called in January. Business was peaking and so was I. In four months I netted Forty Thousand Dollars. In March (1982) I had a 1983 Porsche; the next year's newest model, built in Germany and sent to me.

I kept the majority of my supply stashed in a safe house and brought a workable amount home.

This load was somewhere around four hundred pounds of premium bud with the average bail weighing around forty pounds. They never weighed an exactly even number and so there would be a tag on each bail indicating its invoice number along with the gross package weight and approximate tare, or true content weight. Dependant upon trust and management level this was handled accordingly to insure an exact net number agreed upon. In this high stress business trust was invaluable. It took years to build, but it reduced the stress considerably and made things move along much more quickly.

"Being dirty" is a term we used for having something illegal in possession, whether it was on your person, in your car, in your home or on your property. This might not matter as much to a drug user as it would to a dealer simply because the most a user would have in possession would be his entire stash and a pipe or rolling papers, and generally he would not be holding that much. The conviction for having less than one ounce of marijuana in possession was a misdemeanor with a fine and carried no jail time. A user could afford to be a bit more casual. A dealer had no such luxury. More than an ounce was a whole different story. Being caught in possession of any amount gave legal right to search during that arrest, and a cause for a search warrant to be issued extending the search of your home. If a seed was found in your car's carpet your home could be searched. If you had more than a reasonable amount of cash on you it was suspect and would be confiscated. If the seed was linked to discovering a scale in the home, even if the scale was completely free of residue you could be charged with intent to distribute. Whether it stuck or not, now you were on their radar. You have heat.

To be "clean" meant having nothing illegal or suspect anywhere or in any way connected to your life. That was a rare and welcomed relief.

I think typically inside each successful marijuana dealer is a ticking clock, and eventually you want to be long gone before it buzzes. Carefulness is a premium necessity. Quick performance is a welcomed second.

I would take one bail at a time to my bigger dealers and then one or two home to break down for the smaller dealers to handle. You never want to be caught with the whole load by the police or have someone rob one location and get all your hooch. You never trust anyone with everything. You never share information. You never allow any introductions. You never meet with more than one person, never letting anyone bring a girlfriend or partner. You never have any money on you or at the location where you stash or while making a shipment. You never call house to house, and you never say anything that could be incriminating, even over the payphones. Never use real names in records. Never keep records located on premises, your person, with the stash or with money.

## *Angel in the Basement*

Well, my warehouse was finally empty and I had only two bails now stashed at home to get rid of.

Of course I kept a little personal stash, always less than an ounce of pot, because that's where the law drew the line between user and dealer. My lady had a hand full of diet pills that I insisted she keep in a depleted vitamin B bottle in the cupboard, but what I didn't know was that she also had two loose Quaaludes just sitting there as well that morning.

Sean was a smalltime dealer that I would toss the odd amount to when he was hungry. I had a pound of pot hid in the bottom of my bedroom closet for him to pick up that day.

I rolled home in my Porsche at about 5:30 that morning from a bachelor party at the Italian American Club which involved drinking booze and snorting cocaine. I was so messed up I lost one of my gold bracelets during that episode and just got in the door and sat on the couch and lit up a Marlboro when there was a knock on the door. It was Detective Clarke and a uniform cop with a search warrant that contained a list of stolen merchandise. That was bad and good in a way. It was bad because I was hung over and had no sleep and the list contained a video cassette player that was hooked up to my TV. My three Doberman Pinchers were now barking and I volunteered to let them loose in the back yard so the cops could enter our home.

Detective Clarke explained to me that a junkie rolled me over as a buyer of the stolen merchandise naming this guy John who I did buy it from, and his girl friend Joan as the connection. This was true. I met Joanie sometime back at Hoover's Bar and took a liking to her. Her boyfriend John I didn't know personally and didn't associate with his crowd because they were marked for trouble, but petite pretty women are my Achellies heel and Joanie was charming. Whenever I would run into her at a club or the bar she would be alone or with another girl. I never saw her out with her boyfriend, but she would often tell me how he was trying to straighten out his life and needed a break, how he wanted to work for me and how they would appreciate anything I could do for them.

John got his chance one night while I was hanging out drinking at a packed club called the Lighthouse outside of my regular turf without a bodyguard. I was getting my drinks from a cute little dark haired waitress named Stacy and John and Joanie happened to be there together that night. John was a good looking young man with a body builder's physique. We said hello and they slipped on to the dance floor disappearing into the fray.

As I was holding my drink and listening to the music a big fellow bumped into me almost spilling my drink. I thought nothing of it as the place was quite crowded, so I just moved over a few steps. Then it happened again. This time I was facing the bar with my back turned to the guy. I carefully looked over my right shoulder to see if this was going to turn into something worse and magically the guy was gone. Then in about five minutes John quick steps himself up to me and states "I took care of that for you."

"Took care of what?" I asked

"That guy, I saw him bump you. He was looking for trouble so I took him outside and gave him some. He won't be back."

"Thanks, I'll remember that." I said. John looked content, having had the opportunity, he made the right impression on me.

It was maybe a month or so later that I received a call from Joanie explaining that John was having financial difficulties and was selling some of his stuff to pay off his debts and would I at least look at his video cassette player. They were at least $500 new at that time and all he wanted was $100 for his. I took the bate thinking to return him the favor. Joanie gave me directions to John's home where I met them and his cousin. I gave him cash for the unit and brought it home and connected it to my TV. That was a week before the knock on the door.

On the inside I'm praying "God please don't let me get busted! Please don't let me get busted!

I don't want to go to jail! I can't go to jail. Please don't let me go to jail!"

I know I have a lot more here at stake than a stolen video tape player. I have a pound of reefer in the bedroom closet plus some head stash on my shelf, a .22 caliber rifle and a shotgun in the same closet, $850 in cash in my briefcase under my bed with my coded black book, a bottle of uppers in the kitchen pantry and much bigger problems down stairs. I'm holding client's .375 magnum with papers for ransom on a reefer deal in a dresser. I got a .38 police special with no papers inside the back panel of my clothes washer and we're just beginning to get warm.

On the floor to the right of the stairs are two black plastic garbage bags. Empty they weigh 112 grams each. It's my business to know that. But they're not empty. One has potting soil in it for Roxanne's house plants and flowers. The other is full of the wrappers I stripped form bails of marijuana that came from Columbia. They still smelled like reefer and were originally designed to hold chicken feed for Columbia farmers. I knew that because they were covered with the words "Chicken Feed" in Spanish and with red silhouettes of chickens. Worse than that, they had strips of duct tape, which is good for everything especially criminal activities, that had writing in black marker indicating the bail's invoice number and its gross and tare weights. And, I had lots of them stuffed in that bag. So what am I doing holding that? Well there's an answer for everything we did.

As I stated before "being dirty' or "holding" was a highly dangerous and therefore a highly stressful situation. Marijuana was particularly difficult to conceal. The faster this hot potato dispersed into oblivion the harder it would be to pinpoint its present location and to follow its trail backward. A calculated risk of trust was worth a lot in terms of handling time.

## *Wrappers*

Ultimately the success of a black market business lies with trust and integrity. It is a major part of the risk factor, and as in any business the trust is built on a history of shared experience, and it comes in handy when moving a quarter ton of contraband.

Time and experience produce a useful consistency reducing stress when each link in the chain is well rehearsed with the former and the later link. Example; when the same crew is wrapping the product it becomes apparent that they naturally use the same amount of packaging material per bundle and the tare weight of this material becomes consistent. Also if they have a history of repeat business it is due largely to their honesty. Attempts have been made to cheat by adding heavy objects in the middle of the bail. Once we found a hammer head tucked in a bag. On another occasion the center of the bail was mostly hollowed and filled with several pounds seeds that had shaken off in handling. You don't want to be responsible for such deception.

There are legitimate discrepancies as well. Sometimes on a water drop; that's when you coordinate an airplane with a go-fast boat, the vinyl outer layer of the package may leak and the inner paper product will absorb several pounds of water weight.

Good trust business partners save time and freshness by passing off the bails in the original wrappers checking all the gross weights and stripping the wrappers completely off of only a few bails to verify the net figure. Records are kept down the line and if a discrepancy should occur each handler keeps his trash in a garbage bag of known weight and can produce it if necessary. This is important because the average wrapper is around three and a half pounds. If for example the average bail is forty pounds and you have ten bails, you are carrying thirty five pounds of paper. At the bail price of $350 you have a potential discrepancy of $12,250 over paper.

It is equally incriminating to have such wrappers in possession and the goal is to be able to meet for lunch or call payphone to payphone and in code agree that the "tires were right for the car". Then the wrappers can be disposed of.

In the market place Marijuana was valued by quality and sold by weight. In the 1970s quality was vastly varied and was an extremely interesting part of the business. Many factors come into play to insure quality from cultivation to packaging. Marijuana has a shelf life. It does loose potency. For now let's consider the weight factor. Shrinkage and drying can cause several difficulties most of which are managed by proper packaging, handling and shipping.

From the farm source I have been privy to three major forms of packaging. First and crudest was the burlap bail. Most of the reefer I was experienced with in the early days came from Mexico in burlap bails. It was highly exposed to external conditions. Sometimes it got wet weighing more and losing potency, and sometimes it dried out and powdered losing weight and potency. Either way there was spoilage along with that tell tail smell that traveled everywhere the reefer went. But usually this particular grade was so cheap that there was plenty of room to adjust the price. Then again that same margin allowed for cheating.

When the "Boys" saw a market that there organized skills could profit from they lent a hand in managing smuggling in volume as professionals. This widely connected and diverse organization utilized other tools they already had access or control of including cigarettes. Tobacco had many of the same properties and package and handling problems solved. I would have enjoyed being a fly on the wall in the garage, restaurant, or board meeting where these solutions were discussed. Ultimately what I do remember is that the reefer that came from the direction of the city was pressed into boxes originally made to contain large numbers of cartons of cigarettes. I know this because the large boxes looked like giant packs of smokes displaying the various popular tobacco labels on the entire surface area of each suitcase sized box. Uniform sized boxes traveled well in containers on ships and in trailer trucks. Pressing the product reduced the size per weight ratio but traveling from South America on ship took time and the product dried out often yielding a lot of useless dust. It was called commercial grade lumbo by the handlers. We called it "Dirt Weed". It was moved in hundreds, even thousands of tons.

Everything about the best made it the best. It was garden quality. I mean it was cared for like the Colombian coffee portrayed in the old TV commercials showing the fictional Alex Sijente hand picking each bean only when it was at its ripest. The "Gold" was planted high in the mountains closest to the sun where the days were long and the air, the water, and the soil was the freshest. And oh yes! It was essential that the buds were selected and picked at the perfect moment. Too early and the THC level is not fully realized. Too late and the THC degrades into another less powerful compound. The rest of the plant was useless. The select buds were carefully packed like nuggets of cereal in brown paper feed bags. These bags went into another brown paper feed bag and again into a third brown paper feed bag. These feed bags were tightly wrapped in the heavy duty green and black vinyl garbage bags taped closed with duct tape. Then they were carried to a mountain air strip, weighed and numbered and air lifted by a refueled private plane. From this point two plans showed great success. The first was to drop below radar at some point and rendezvous with a "cigarette" boat (so called for its long narrow hull) or other "go fast" boat and air drop the hooch into the water. The plane would continue on to land empty inside the U.S. border while the pleasure boat mingled with the sea traffic or made a bee line for the shore. The risks were high. Traveling low in the water could bring attention and loud powerful boats in the night could draw suspicion. There is also the danger of pirates catching a glimpse of the maneuvers and attempting to heist the booty.

Our preferred option was to land the loaded plane in the southern U.S. refuel and continue north eventually getting lost on the radar scope between mountains in the northeast. At this point an identically labeled airplane would take off between the mountains and rendezvous below radar with the packed plane, then climb out with the loaded plane making one radar blip until they passed into another pair if mountains where the loaded plane dropped out of sight and the empty plane would continue on to another state and log into a small airport empty.

It took only five minutes to unload three tons of reefer by fork lift. Again the hot potato passed to stash houses and my partner would get the call. He would grab our chunk and stash it, then we would meet and I would take my load to my warehouse and continue to work as quickly and as secretly as possible until every speck was gone with the every trace of scent. Only then could I breathe.

I am not quite up to the point of taking that deep free breath when the knock came to my door. So while I'm praying hard on the inside, on the outside I'm cool as a cucumber taking long slow puffs on my cigarette buying time to size everything up between questions and play my best role as a good guy in town who custom paints motorcycles and portraits and got bedazzled by a pretty girl.

After Detective Clarke gave me the scoop on John and Joanie and was showing me the warrant with a long list of stolen merchandise I knew the best thing to do was to act innocent, a little surprised and polite. Maybe I could get them out of the house quickly before they picked up a scent of what really was going on with me. I pointed to the video player and offered it to them.

They obliged, but Clarke was prepared. He again pointed to the list of stolen goods citing a camera and some pearls and jewelry stating that the rat said I might have them as well and since they were on the warrant they were going to go ahead and look everywhere in the house for them as well all the while watching my eyes and body language for a clue.

I may have been a bit slow from the drug hang over and not sleeping but I got the picture. I remember that I gave John and Joan a taste of coke at his house when I picked up the video player and the cousin was lurking around. The rat was looking at jail time and that means no heroin, so he gives up all he got. He doesn't really know what I do so he make me out to be a coke dealer.

Clarke was looking for coke. That too was good and bad. The warrant gave him access, our house was fair game now, but a large garbage bag wasn't a likely place to stash cocaine in this lower middle class converted bungalow, even if a Porsche was outside, the whole picture didn't quite fit that profile. No, if this guy had any cocaine it would be in a zip lock sandwich bag in the refrigerator or a coffee can, maybe in his clothes or dresser, something on that level. Fortunately for me that was how he set his sights, but he wasn't going to leave any stone unturned.

Clarke explained that Roxanne had to stay in one place with the uniform officer while he took me all around the house room by room. That way we couldn't get a step ahead of them and he could use me, the suspect, as a tell-tail. You remember when you were a kid, while your friend searched about you would say "You're getting warmer, warmer… colder, colder." You get my drift. To get a feel for my truth-or-lie line, he asks if I have any drugs or anything illegal here. I of course casually deny any such thing.

So we leave the now disconnected VCR on the dining room table and Clarke wants to search the bedroom where he starts going over the shelves.

He finds the plastic container with my personally selected "head stash", premium gold buds and shaking the container in my face he raises his voice saying "What is this? I thought you said you didn't smoke pot!"

"What did you want me to say; 'I smoke a little?'"

Then he goes through my closet and pulls out a twelve gauge shotgun and a .22 caliber rifle tossing them on the bed. Digging deeper he finds a whole one pound bag of reefer. "What about this?" He barks.

"Look I paint a lot of motorcycles" I explain calmly. "I took a small deposit on a paint job from some guy in Newark who never paid me for the work. The he shows up three months later and says "I can give you a pound of pot for the balance." I figure it will take me at least a year to smoke it and I won't have to associate with any drug dealers, so I took it. I forgot it was even there."

Clarke tosses that on the bed with the head stash and guns. "This is starting to look bad." I am thinking when he reaches under the bed and pulls out my old attaché that was my dad's when he was Mayor. Tossing that on the edge of the bed he pops open the latches and finds eight hundred dollars in cash lying inside. "How much is that?" he asks.

"Eight hundred and change." I answer.

"That's a lot of money to have hanging around."

I'm thinking he has no idea forty two thousand in cash is still hiding.

"What are you doing with that kind of money?"

"I sell Shaklee Vitamins." I answer."

"Then where are the vitamins?"

"I'm out of stock." I say "That's why I have the cash."

Realizing that he is buying it, I slowly expel a sigh of relief.

His eyes are back in the case and he pulls out my coded black book. It contains enough information to put me away for a while: transactions, weights and cash balances.

"What do we got here?" he asks as he flips the pages back and forth.

"That is the sales and orders for the Shaklee Vitamins."

"Oh." Clarke tossed the book back in the case with the cash and close the lid.

All the while I am still praying "God please don't let me go to jail."

Now we go into the kitchen and his first target is the refrigerator. I know he has been looking for cocaine all along. That has to be what the rat told him to look for and that is actually in my favor today. He then opens all the cabinets and the cupboard and picks up two loose Quaaludes that Roxanne had left there. My lips draw tight because she knows the rules.

"What are these?"

"I don't know, Tylenol." I act like I'm guessing.

"They're Quaaludes, soapers, that's what they are." He replies, and picks up a brown Shaklee B-Complex bottle and rattling it he asks the same question.

"Shaklee B-complex." I say.

This time Roxanne got it right by putting her twenty amphetamine tablets into a labeled bottle.

The detective returns them to the shelf.

Our house is an old fashioned Cape Cod with real clapboard siding. It also has the bathroom off the kitchen where the detective searches next. Nothing incriminating is found there. Right next to the bathroom door is the door to the basement. Detective Clarke looks at me bewildered and says "We're done here." I hope I have hidden my feeling of relief and we leave the kitchen and bath area and return to the living where he asks about the second floor. I explain that Roxanne's children stay there and we climb the steps. He finds a crawlspace in the eves and finding nothing there we return to the first floor. Looking to the uniform officer he says "I think we are done here." Then reconsidering he takes me back to the door in the kitchen that leads down to the basement. Again he is off balance and says "We don't have to go there." Again he reconsiders and decides to search there as well.

In the basement to the left is a chest of drawers. Behind the dresser up in a hollow in between the concrete blocks and the wall frame is a small safe with forty two thousand dollars in cash, mostly in hundred dollar bills. But he misses it. Searching one drawer at a time from the top he finds nothing in the first, nothing in the second, nothing in the third, and in the fourth; a .357 magnum pistol with registration in the name of a customer. It is not loaded and I explain that my buddy and I went to a pistol range. When we returned to my house we had some drinks and felt it best to leave the weapon until we met again sober. Clarke bought the line but explained that he would have to take the pistol and contact the owner to verify the story and return it.

Close by was our washer and dryer. Inside the back of the dryer I kept a .38 revolver. It was not discovered. I could see that the detective was very uncomfortable in this basement. Maybe because I am standing behind him and to his right most of the time because the ceiling is low and the space is tight, and maybe God is protecting me somehow.

At the foot of the stairs against the wall were those two vinyl garbage bags. He is looking at them as I am praying, and yeah, I see his pistol on his right hip, maybe that makes him uncomfortable having me behind him an arms length from his pistol. No good could come from that move.

Clarke asks "What's in that bag?"

"Dirt." I answer. "Roxanne grows all kinds of flowers and plants. It's potting soil."

"Not that bag. The other one."

"Garbage." I answer. "You want to see."

"No." Clarke is stirring uncomfortably. I send a "thank you" up to God.

That bag had the wrappers with Spanish writing, bail lot numbers and the gross and net weights for several bails of pot totaling a hundred and eighty pounds.

I feel a presence and look around the basement carefully. My work space is a walled off cubicle to my right, behind the stairs, and has only a drape hanging in the open doorway to separate it from full view.

Beyond the draped doorway is a small eight by ten workroom with a wooden workbench against the far wall easily visible from the entrance. Under the bench lies a bail of marijuana and a box containing a lab scale, accurate to the fraction of a gram with a capacity above a kilo. On a shelf across from the bench is another box containing a scale for large packages, It is accurate to a quarter of an ounce and has a two hundred pound capacity.

I see the closed drape, there is nothing there that my eyes can see, yet I see a man with his arms crossed and his legs shoulder width apart. His presence is guarding the doorway. Clarke is not looking there, it is as if he is unable to. He appears more flustered, maybe even scared.

We turn from the bags on the floor now to the shelved wall on the right. The shelves are narrow containing my spray paint gun and an eclectic cache of things stored and forgotten.

Clarke keeps me on his right side as he peruses the shelves removing various items and examining them. My body is the only visible thing between the detective and the draped doorway. On the floor below the shelves is a group of large cardboard boxes storing larger items. He is not interested in them. He is looking for something small. The detective's toes are an inch away from such a box that he uses to table smaller boxes from the shelves and open them searching their contents. He never opens this box. It was used to store a large flat window fan, but not lately. Today it had a thirty seven pound bail of pot inside, but he is looking for something hiding cocaine. He has me unscrew the paint cup and air cap off of the spray gun. It is empty.

Clarke's nerves unravel again as he turns left and right in confusion. My angel is still standing guard at the draped doorway to the last bail.

"We're through here." Clarke says, and points up the stair case, "Let's go."

They grab the two rifles, the magnum with the registration, the pound of pot and the head stash with the two Quaaludes and the video tape player. They leave my cash and black book and the detective explains that he doesn't want to make a scene so I can walk uncuffed to the unmarked car outside while they load the trunk. I agree.

Roxanne is not charged at this time and is left behind to call our attorney as I am carted off to the police station.

During the interrogation the detective explains that if this guy gave me one whole pound of pot without breaking it up into ounces that it was likely that he had more; maybe five pounds, possibly ten. I would just be getting another dealer off the street by cooperating.

While he is speaking I'm seeing the two bails floating one over each of his shoulders almost amusingly.

"Taking him out wouldn't stop the flow of marijuana in New Jersey, believe me." He states.

"You have no idea what this does to the flow in three states." I'm thinking as I lower my head and side to side indicating "No."

"I can't do that. I don't really know this guy."

It might have been a feather in his cap but Clarke's real agenda is solving the "Break and entry" crimes and that make today a good one for him.

He rehearses the whole truth about John, Joanie and the third guy and asks only for a statement to the effect that they brought me the offer of the goods. I agree and am booked for possession of stolen property, possession of marijuana and fingerprinted. Clarke thanks me for my cooperation and releases me without bail.

I thanked God knowing that this could have gone much worse for me. Right now I have not even been charged with "intent to distribute". But my problems are not nearly over yet. I'm still holding seventy plus pounds, I have dealers owing me their balances, and I owe ninety thousand dollars to my supplier.

While I was off to the police station Roxanne was acting intelligently and heroically. She gathered up her laundry in two piles and one at a time put a bail in her laundry basket wrapped and covered in clothes and brought the bails to my Camaro in the driveway. Dressed in her work uniform Roxanne drove that car to her work place as normal. Using the payphone Roxanne called my buddy who maintains my cars and while she worked as usual, he arrived in the night and took the

Camaro to a stash house we had in another town, emptied the contents and returned the car without incident.

By the grace of God I had never been arrested before and I therefore qualified for a Pretrial Intervention Program offered to first offenders whereby I was fined and not tried but put on probation for a year with the stipulation that if I kept my record clean I could and did have my arrest record expunged.

On the other side though, the vultures were gathering. One guy tried to play me. I had work to do and I moved one bail to a good man. But someone greedy is always there to play you when you are vulnerable. My pal from the sunshine state fronted as a real estate broker but he reeked of being a conman. He had done one really solid turn a year ago and might deserve the benefit of a doubt but I knew better, and, better than my instincts were those of Roxanne. She could smell a rat at a proven 1500 miles away and often warned me that this guy stank.

I met Cosmo the Russian more than a year ago through a local small time player who had big ambitions. He showed up at our first meet looking like he just got off the set of Miami Vice. He had the talk and acted like the world ate out of his hand. Cosmo made his conquests by being charming. He was all smoke and mirrors but it worked enough for him to keep him in play. What I liked was that he had the legitimate business side well insulated. Florida was booming all over and he was taking deposits. To gain my confidence he offered me a connection that he had in Boston that was for real and professional. Tommy Goodman was an architect in love with a girl ten years younger than him and was as precise as his tools and as honorable as Abe Lincoln. We worked business on the payphones and met in NYC to consummate our deal; it went down as smooth as silk. But Tommy had a warning for me. "If you want to pay Cosmo for the connection that is your business, but I am telling you truthfully he is worthless. He didn't hold up his end before and I believe he won't again."

I answered "He brought us together and I will compensate him for that." which I did. Tommy and I made a considerable amount of money together. That played into the equation.

From then on Cosmo smelled money on me so about six months before Detective Clarke showed up at the door Cosmo contacted me with a shaky plan to sell me a quarter pound of cocaine. I didn't have to explain it again that I didn't deal in cocaine, and the only reason I was listening to this story was because he gave me Goodman, and Goodman was sterling. Yet Tommy Goodman's voice was reminding me "This guy is no good." Backing that was my partner's word of wisdom when he and I began our relationship "Just sell one thing." But Cosmo's charm was just intoxicating enough for me to give him another chance at success.

Maybe he had more Tommy Goodmans in his pocket.

Roberto worked for me for years, he was faithful and astute. He had a long time association with Freddy Tyler whose main industry was party packages of coke. His business was small enough to keep him from getting hurt by the junkies or bigger dealers, and by the law. He had a real job cover and a clean record, and he operated outside of my realm. I could check the quality and front the five grand, let Freddy pick-up the package do his cut and distribute and pay me back with profit. At least I could fly south and peak at the product.

I told Cosmo that I was busy, business was good and I didn't need to get involved with something else right now. I heard a little desperation in his voice and what got me was having a soft heart when someone was down. So I put my life on hold and flew to Florida with five grand cash in hand and met with Cosmo. As I had guessed his story was nonsense. "That stuff is gone, but I got another guy…" Finally after a couple of days he came up with a taste of some real garbage since I decided to head home. Of course what he really wanted was to get his hands on the five k and he wasn't shy about asking to borrow it. Against my good judgment I lent it to him.

So back to the present situation, I'm released from police custody and send one of the bails off to a dependable associate. Meanwhile

Cosmo is trying to pay back the five k and he gets another shot at me while I'm staggering.

"Come up to Boston, I got a place outside of town in a country setting where we can hang out and you won't feel the heat. You can get your thoughts together. By the way if you are holding, I could use the work to help pay you back."

I took one last risk with Cosmo and paid my driver to deliver the final bail to him and his man. Over the next month I got all my money back from the five grand loan I gave him and I was almost paid up on the bail. He and his man came up $1500 short and I knew it grew wings.

Cosmo was making a drive from Florida back to his home up north and stopped at my house in a preowned Mercedes Benz he just bought and hands me another $300 while he tells me "I got to feed my family." And now I have a choice to make. Start a small war or take the hit and cut him off. I chose the second.

Frankie Fontana looked like he was straight from a doo-wop group. He had a dark pompadour hair style and wore blue sun glasses at all times. They gave him a mysterious look while hiding his slightly "Marty Feldmon eyes". He had that bite where his bottom teeth closed in front of the top teeth making his jaw jut forward adding a very slight lisp to his breathy whisper of a voice that often sounded like a sigh of pain.

Frankie literally broke his back when, as a policeman, he was chasing a liquor store robber and slipped on ice and fell. He had discs removed and rods inserted and he could walk okay but was always in some pain and lost a lot of flexibility. Apparently he got a bad deal with early retirement and tried to be a plumber, believe it!

But Frankie's world had him connected to a cocaine dealer in New York that paid him to drive him and his associates around. Part of the gratis was a sizable personal package of pure Peruvian flake which he pieced out to a small circle of friends in New Jersey.

We met in the late 1970s through such a mutual friend. I would buy the flake off him and share it with my crew around the holidays.

Eventually Frankie's associates got pinched and ratted each other out. Frankie was way too small to get noticed and only found himself without a job again. Since my business was booming and could use another good soldier, I offered him work driving bails across state lines with his pistol, CB, and Police Ban radio on. He had a big blue Caddy with a huge trunk and a Police Shield displayed in the rear window. He was a seasoned man. He was safe, proven, and loyal.

I also fronted Frankie as many pounds as he could sell at a rate that made him a profit.

After the bust I was running scared. I began pounding coke up my nose like a madman, and using valium, Quaaludes or alcohol to try and level out. I'd freak out if I smoked any weed. It amplified my fears. This was not the life I wanted.

I hated being home and I hated being alone. I was always in a running away mode. I kept at least three different cars full of gas in different locations in case I detected a need to escape, real or imagined. On one such a night I drove the Porsche over to Bobby E's. He looked like Chris Christopherson with a gimp he acquired from a motorcycle accident. That got him hooked on Percocets which he counteracted with crystal meth. His lovely wife loved the crank. They had no problem staying up for hours sharing the speed with alcohol and an occasional Quaalude while we made ourselves heroes.

Sufficiently loaded I determined I needed to fly to Fort Lauderdale to cool out. It was 4:00a.m. when I headed out to the airport. In those days all you needed to board a flight was money. Jet travel was like taking a bus. I got a room at a Ho-Jo's on the beach and don't remember the rest until the flight back where I met Nancy the nurse. She traded seats with the guy next to me so we could smoke and chat. When we landed we grabbed my Porsche and headed to my cabin cruiser in south Jersey. We had a seafood dinner at the Captain's Inn with a wonderful bottle of wine and a joint, sex on the beach and the boat as well, and headed to wherever it was that she lived in N.J. as long as it was far enough from me. We partied at a local tavern where she showed me off to the locals and I disappeared into the night just like in the movies.

A few days later I showed up at Frankie's. We discussed some business sniffed some coke off of his coffee table with a rolled up Hundred, and talked like guys do. Frankie looked at me with his big smile and said, "James, you're what every man wants to be! You got the Batmobile" referring to my black Porsche parked below his apartment window, "You got a beautiful woman, money, and the hair…" Back then I had a full head of well-groomed hair. "You got the clothes" he continued on.

Sitting on the couch hovering over the lines of cocaine on the table, I took a deep breath. "Frankie" I said "you see that Porsche outside? It's an '83. This is 1982. It isn't even brand new yet! And I'm already looking at another model. I have a thirty-five foot cabin cruiser and I'm looking at forty-footer. I have a three bedroom one bath house with a basement. I want two baths and a garage. You see this line of coke?" measuring it with my two index fingers, "It's this long. I want it to be" tripling the distance between my two index fingers "*this* long." I leaned back into the couch. "You know someone once asked John D. Rockefeller in an interview, 'John, how much is enough?'" (Now Rockefeller's fortune in today's money would equal an estimated one hundred billion dollars.)

"Do you know what his answer was Frankie?" raising my right hand up to our eye level and closing one eye, I peaked with the other through about a quarter inch of space between my thumb and index finger "' Just a little more!' he said, "Just a little more'!" I stood up and groping the air explained, "The devil is ten feet in front of me dangling a carrot and walking backwards to a cliff. I don't have a hundred million dollars. I don't even have one million, but I know already there is never 'Just a little more!' There is never enough!" I decided then I wasn't going to live like this anymore.

It took one more event to seal the deal. I went on another coke tare. That's when I would buy an ounce of really pure coke and kid myself that I could sell off some before I consumed the whole thing. After doing up the first eight ball I got my facts straight: I don't sell coke, you could get busted selling coke, I consume it!

It's early evening and my phone rings. Dennis is at a bar two miles away wanting some blow. Good! I can recover a hundred or two and get away from staring at the bag. I drive over and have one drink. We do the deal and Dennis offers me a toot. Wisdom would say "no" but I can't. We load up huge blasts each off of a match book cover and I start heading home before it takes full effect.

The event I am describing took place twenty three years ago (from the time I wrote this portion), but the effects of drug addiction are so profound that I had to stop typing and relieve my bowels a moment ago. I am offering this information to give to my readers some insight into drug use outside the prescribed boundaries of medicine and law.

When drugs are administered by a physician or anesthesiologist, or taken strictly in prescribed form, the effects are somewhat predictable. Self-medicating or recreational use is another world. Hence the popular term from the 1960's: "experimenting".

One of those effects unique to sniffing or "snorting" cocaine manifests during a 'coke tare' or 'run' when the compulsive use goes on for days. I shall call this type of episode, ***The Perfect Storm!***

Phase one, ***Building Winds:*** The situation is physical and takes place in the nose and sinuses. The chronic packing of abrasive chemicals in the nasal membrane (tissue) cause swelling, scabbing and "crusting" in the passages. The human body perceives that it is being attacked and attempts to defend itself. The porous membrane eventually becomes blocked as a pasty mixture of blood mucus and cocaine glaze it over. That's what is happening physically.

***Second Storm:*** Mentally another storm is brewing.

Obviously, as with all addictions, tolerance builds up with use. Also characteristically cocaine affects the brain quickly. The effect is called the "Rush." Basically what is happening chemically in the brain is that the neurotransmitters are saturated with the drug which resembles the brain's natural pleasure producing chemicals such as serotonin and dopamine. This flood creates a feeling of euphoria. As the drug quickly metabolizes out the pleasure leaves, or the "high" wears off. This effect is known as the "Crash." But this does not leave the brain in the same state as it was before the drug use. Rather the brain is depleted not only of the cocaine but also now has a diminished supply of its own natural pleasure producing chemicals since they were replaced by the cocaine ingestion.

As the brain crashes it sounds the alarm that it needs the drug. The voice of reason (originating in the cerebral cortex) says "Stop and endure the crash. The drug can no longer be affective." But the craving (which originates in the Hypothalamus) loudly insists on being gratified. Panic sets in as the war for sanity begins to rumble.

Here the Hypothalamus, which is a more primitive part of the brain, usurps authority over the rational mind subjecting it to plan for more drug consumption. Now all kinds of compulsive behaviors kick in: Pick your nose, blow your nose, douche it with warm water, take a steaming shower, and my favorite; drill through the blockage with another whopping line of coke! Oh yeah, or you *could* wait twenty minutes then try it again, but… you are in the **Perfect Storm!**

I have vodka in me and a huge blast of coke starting to come on as I drive home. By the time I'm in the door my heart is pounding in my ears. I'm panicking! Thoughts race, "Don't move too fast or exert…don't sit down… sit down… whoa! I'm shaking. How much do I have in my system! How much is melting in my sinuses!" I sit on the edge of my bathtub. Sweat is actually running out of both palms. "Don't breathe too fast! Don't stop breathing!" My ears are ringing and I have tunnel vision, and my heart feels like it is leaving my chest. THE MOMENT OF TRUTH HAS COME. "God, please don't let me die! Please don't let me die! I don't want to live like this anymore. I don't want to live like this. Take all of this away from me. Take my life and use it for something good. Save me!"

Roxanne would come quietly and ask if she should call 911. My life might be saved, but I'd be staring at a bust. "Wait." Is all I could mutter each time she asked.

Slowly, slowly with intermitting gasps reminding me to breathe, I began to come down from the drug, and it took hours, sitting on the edge of the tub praying for God to change my life.

**He did.**

I don't remember how long I took to recover but when I felt well enough I called the closest Porsche dealer in the area and offered my car. They put it on their showroom floor. I bought an old used Chevy station wagon with 99,000 miles on it. I watched as the odometer lapped itself back to zero miles. I called Charlie Bonnet the realtor. A sign went up in front of the house.

Seeing the sign, my next door neighbor asked, "What are you going to do with the boat?"

"Sell it"

"It must be worth a lot." She replied curiously.

"What do you got?"

Shyly looking down, "Oh, only about twelve hundred dollars." She said softly with no expectation.

"Sold" I replied.

## *Of Mice and Men*

My partner and I were now playing a very high stakes game. Progressive risks over the years brought larger rewards, but the rewards never matched the risks, and I did have somewhat of a moral compass, some call a conscience, others call Him Holy Spirit. This tugging meant more to me that the fear factor. I challenged my fears and enjoyed conquering them. That is how I got this far in this business, but the belief in God gave purpose to my life. Otherwise what was all this nonsense for? I wasn't motivated to quit because it was illegal and I had never thought it was wrong to sell or smoke pot, yet now things were changing rapidly. It was an opportunity to reexamine my character and my goals, and, like I cried from the bathroom tub "I don't want to live like this anymore!"

My partner had his eyes on the prize. All the hard work we had done brought the top dogs in position to retire millionaires. Now it would be our turn. He and I would own the route and the plane. We would run the game. There was nothing above us but blue sky and a twin engine airplane that could carry three tons of marijuana. If we worked for one more year we could retire well.

I was making other plans.

## *The Plan*

You have to have a plan. My spiritual eyes were yet untrained and dark. The good news is that the God of the Universe knows this, and He makes "All things work together for good for them that love *Him*, to them that are the called according to His purpose." (Romans 8:28) God would respond to my honest heart's cry.

My Catholic upbringing taught that living intimately unmarried together was a sin and displeasing to God. I knew that was true for all Christian faiths in general. I knew Roxanne loved me faithfully and waited patiently for seven years for our relationship to mature. It was time. I was hoping that if I made this right in God's sight it would please Him and a window of opportunity might open for us to fall in love again and find the plan He truly had for us. I could not admit to myself that I wasn't in love with her. I was hoping for a miracle. This seemed to me to be right up His ally. I shared all this with Roxanne, including my desire to look at our lives from God's perspective. Roxanne had inside herself a faith in Jesus that supported her throughout many years of trials which included coming from a family of ten children and losing her father also when she was fourteen. She would be happy to leave the road we were on to travel one of enlightenment, and she would be happy to be my wife.

We were in the fast lane planning our wedding as well as our escape. On April 17, 1983 we tied the knot in a Catholic Church in Pompton

Plains where I knew a priest. We honeymooned in Acapulco and had to give away a pair of earrings to guarantee us a plane ride home. Corruption was everywhere.

Our next step was to move to Hollywood Beach Florida where I had put a deposit, against the advice of my new attorney, on an Italian restaurant on Route One, about one mile from the beach. What a mistake. Or was it?

Two years later my pastor, Terry Bomar would ask "What's the worst thing that could have happened?"

Astonished I realized, "Nothing."

Let me explain. What did happen was that I never opened the restaurant. Suspecting the owners were "wise guys" my attorney hired a private investigator to check into the licenses and background of the business and the owners. His suspicions were correct. The liquor license was a 4COPSRX license. That translates as a "special restaurant license" which allows the establishment to serve any type of alcohol on the premises until 4:00 am providing that the dining area has seating and table space to serve meals to a particular number of persons. This business had a dance floor giving it a more club type atmosphere in order to sell more liquor until 4:00am. But even if the dance floor had been used for dining space I still doubt that it would meet the required table minimum for the restaurant liquor license status. For the wise guys the simple solution was to pay off the inspector.

I was determined not to begin my new career on the wrong foot after all the hiding I had done for the last thirteen years, so on the advise of my attorney I sued the sellers for misrepresentation. They in turn countered with a suit for failure to perform the contract. They were well aware that I would settle out of court rather than be tied up in the courts for a year spending money on attorneys and legal fees. I would agree to forfeit my escrow deposit.

The picture became clear. This is how that family made their money. They would buy up a liquor license find a somewhat suitable location, make only basic improvements and open the place up by any means necessary all the while putting the "established business" on the market.

Next they would wine and dine an eager buyer convincing him or her to quickly deposit a down payment in escrow with their attorney before someone else snatches up this deal, even offering to hold a note on the balance.

The naive buyer takes possession and spends additional sums on improvements. Then when the business lags, (since it was never established) the sellers would offer to finance it with interest. If the new owner didn't take the bait and the business failed, it would revert back to the original owners with all the improvements and return on the market with a new face lift ready to lure in the next victim. These wise guys could make fifty to one hundred thousand dollars a year on the *business* without ever opening the door.

To answer the question, "What's the worst thing that could have happened?" simply, if nothing went wrong with the purchase of the restaurant I doubt that I would be living my life for Jesus Christ today, but the failure to complete the transaction with the wise guys put me in the perfect position, both spiritually and geographically, to change the course of my life.

After my life changing experience of letting everything go in this world to follow the plan that God would have for my live, I was renting a house in Hollywood Beach Florida a short distance from the restaurant I lost my deposit on. Roxanne took a job as a waitress at the Hollywood Beach Hilton Hotel and eventually I got a job there parking cars for tips with eighteen year old kids. There was one guy there older than me. Lonnie Tolbert was in his forties and looked better than great for his age. He was an attractive black man with a singing voice that excelled Smokey Robinson's. He had an imperfection that was only noticeable when he shook hands. Both of his hands turned outward at a 45 degree angle like duck feet. No they weren't webbed, they only turned out, but he did suffer the loss of strength to his grip yet he was quite capable of strumming a guitar that he often brought out at break time. He could tickle the ivories as well. Speaking of ivories, Lonnie had a contagious smile, and he had joy written all over him. He spent his time writing gospel music and courting the lovely Verdell.

Now I was working for pocket change, the money I used to leave for the laundry and forget about was now my sustenance.

Roxanne and I agreed to read the Bible every day which we did separately. I began with the New Testament, the first chapter of the first book; Matthew.

On occasion I would roll myself a joint from the stash I had kept from before the move, and take a couple of hits. Generally I was instantly paranoid and couldn't enjoy the high. I remember flipping through the TV channels and often stopped at Trinity Broadcast Network that had a station within miles of where we now lived, but the main broadcast day came from Santa Anna California where the owners Paul and Jan Crouch with their white heads and big hair smilingly affirmed that Jesus Christ was alive and well, saving souls, healing the sick, and helping the poor and afflicted, exactly as He had always been doing.

Their countenance was undeniable. As a man who risked his freedom on many occasions reading people's faces, it was clear to me, not puzzling in the least, that Paul and Jan were absolutely certain this was true. I could read it in their eyes. In a short time I was exposed through the Trinity Broadcast Network to a multitude of ministries, preachers and teachers of various ages, a variety of denominations, with considerable educations and diverse experiences. I watched in the eyes of each as I listened to their messages and I became more and more convinced that Jesus truly was alive.

As October of 1983 drew to a close people everywhere were preparing to celebrate Halloween. The Christians though had a different take. I lit a joint and puffed on it twice as I surfed the tube for some company and landed again on TBN. The guest speaker was Greg Lourie and his subject was witchcraft. Greg explained that the term *witchcraft* as used in our modern English and in the King James English, comes from the Greek word *Pharmakeia* meaning *to administer drugs*.

Similarly the French word *pharmakon*, according to the Webster's Ninth Collegiate Dictionary translates as: *magic charm, poison, drug*. Here of course is the root of our words *pharmacy* and *pharmaceutical*.

I looked down at the joint in my hand, paused and then tamped it out in the ashtray. "What was I doing? I thought as the drug began to saturate accompanied by the familiar fear. "Am I being possessed by this?"

I thought about it again when I was not under the influence of the drug or the fear and decided to flush my remaining stash down the toilet and begin listening and following the ways of God as I perceived them daily through reading the bible, listening to the different ministers messages with reason and openness, and begin going to church.

*Chapter Twenty-Two*

# A CRUMPLED PIECE OF PAPER

In the subdivision where we now lived in Hollywood Beach the ranch style concrete block homes were arranged in straight lines facing the nicely paved streets. Behind each row of houses was a parallel unpaved road used by the sanitation department for garbage collection. This road was lined with a drainage ditch due to the low level of the costal land. I found this to be ideal for walking Kyrie my Doberman. I discovered long ago dog walking be to a good stress relieving exercise. Now at thirty-one I was facing a career change without any guidance or direction and was deeply considering how my life was to measure up to God's divine plan. I did not know who I was or where I was going, and had no idea what to do next since my plans for the restaurant and bar were squashed, and in light of this new Christian information, that probably wasn't an option pleasing to God either.

It was time to talk to God and think, so I told Kyrie to get her leash which she did as always and we headed out the glass sliding doors and down the sanitation road. I put my life on the table and asked the Almighty Loving God for guidance as I walked awhile.

Now I am not much of a garbage picker and I am actually a tiny bit germ phobic but even so a crumpled piece of paper lying in the ditch caught my eye. My nature told me "Don't pick that up."

Immediately a counter command said, "Pick it up, straighten the paper out and read it." I hesitated uncomfortably finally concluding that in my present situation I really had little to lose and perhaps something to gain. After all I was talking to God. Maybe this is how He will answer me. So I crouched down and reached into the ditch and retrieved the crumpled piece of paper. I stood up and gave it a shake and then carefully brushed the dusty dirt away with my fingers. I stretched the folded page back into shape as best as I could and then began to read "Thy word have I hid in my heart that I might not sin against thee. Psalm119:11" There was some text explaining the scripture reference and then another quote "Thy word is a lamp to my feet and a light to my path. Psalm119:105" I took that message to heart and memorized those two verses that day. You may debate all you want about God speaking clearly or this just being a coincidence, but my heart is absolutely certain;

*"For every one that asketh receiveth; and he that seeketh findeth; and to him that knocketh it shall be opened.*
*Or what man is there of you, whom if his son ask bread, will he give him a stone? Or if he ask a fish, will he give him a serpent?*
*If ye then, being evil, know how to give good gifts unto your children, how much more shall your Father which is in heaven give good things to them that ask him?"* Matthew 7:8-11

I didn't get the whole future laid out for me in detail right then, but I did hear from heaven and I did get my answer. I knew now that the Holy Word of God was exactly and completely what I needed to guide my life. I wholeheartedly followed the rest of the leaf of paper which instructed me how to invite Jesus Christ to be the Lord of my life and save me from my sin and judgment to eternal hell by his gift to me of faith in His word and his accomplished work on the cross paying my punishment.

It did not take long for me to understand that I had been a crumpled piece of paper discarded by dark forces over a heartless world that had no use for the message I would now hold. Yet somebody far greater heard this young man cry in an ally used solely for garbage, a place for things wasted and carelessly tossed away, and bent down into the gutter and plucking up this crushed and filthy unrecognizable mess, carefully and patiently blew off the dust, shook out the dirt and softly rubbed away the creases, restoring and reshaping this parched soul to receive new living words.

## *What was your day like?*

Since Roxanne and I had Roman Catholic roots we agreed together to attend Saint Teresa's Catholic Church which was a short distance from our home. That lasted two weeks. Lorraine's work schedule changed and she was given the Sunday morning breakfast and brunch shift to wait on tables. I took this as an opportunity to demonstrate my commitment to God by getting ready and going to the Sunday Mass on my own. I showered and dressed in my Sunday best and pointed our car in the direction of Saint Teresa's. As I drove I began rehearsing my intention to myself, I thought.

"I'm going to Saint Teresa's" I proudly affirmed silently.

"No you're not." Spoke a voice in my head that sounded exactly like my own thinking voice.

"Yes I am." I reassured myself.

"No you're not." My other thinking voice that I thought was me responded gently.

"Yes Me ..." I began, but I was gently interrupted by what logic dictated was my own thought, with "No, you're not going to Saint Teresa's, you are going past Saint Teresa's to the Assemblies of God Church two blocks farther."

"How about that" I'm thinking more quietly so no one else can hear me "I'm having an argument with myself!" I look around the car.

"Well, people talk to themselves" I recall "that can be healthy." To which I hear.

"Not if you are arguing! That's insane!"

"Oh boy! Who is this now?" I wonder.

"Shut up it's me."

"Right. If you…I say so."

As I begin to think that "This is not good." I reel back to the subject at hand; "driving a car to church. That's one foot in reality, and there it is on the left, Saint Teresa's." I click my blinker on, signaling a left turn and decelerate. I have both hands on the wheel and my brain is telling my hands to steer left into the parking lot but my hands are not getting the message, or more accurately, are not believing that that message is my true intent. I give up the struggle and my whole tense body relaxes. I gently press on the gas pedal and glide passed Saint Teresa's Church. At the end of the second block I signal for a right turn and so proceed into the parking lot of the Hollywood Beach Assemblies of God Church. This is of course out of my comfort zone, and shutting the motor off I pray "God if you want me to be here you have got to somehow show me for sure." I try sneaking in the back if that is possible and quickly learn that sneaking into a well-lit church with a congregation of maybe twenty people is near impossible. The little congregation is standing in worship as I slip in the back side door and attempt to blend into oblivion, but you can't hide from God. So I silently and anxiously prayed "God if You want me to be here You have got to tell me or show me somehow because this is all very strange to me."

Pastor Norman McCutchen was a lovely, tall and slender gentleman in his mid-seventies with a tan complexion from having lived for years in Arizona and was presently residing in South Florida. He spoke in an easy tone as his eyes panned the congregation greeting mine for a moment, and continuing on, began to well up slightly as his voice softened.

"You don't know how it thrills me to see a young man walk into this church on a beautiful Sunday morning like this one and choose to be here to worship rather than doing whatever else he could be doing on such a day. You know," he continued "We are a small church here and we are like a family for each other, so let's just come up here and gather around the altar and we will pray together." He motioned with his hands "Come, come."

I followed the crowd to the altar sheepishly, and Pastor Norman walked gracefully up to each person one by one and prayed gently. He laid his hand on my forehead that day and prayed for me. I really don't recall his words but I felt my chest and knees relax, and I believed that God answered the prayer that I prayed from the back of the church. Pastor Norman welcomed me to the church and hoped to see me again. He did, Sunday after Sunday bringing Roxanne in tow when she was not working.

In a short time Norman and his wife returned to Arizona and a rather young Pastor Richard Impellizari, and his beautiful wife Rosanne from New York, took the reins of the Hollywood Beach Assemblies of God. By his request I designed the new church business card; Revelation 1:7 "He cometh with clouds…" in blue on white.

Amazingly the Holy Spirit moved on both Roxanne and me so as to keep us yoked together.

One could easily imagine a relationship being torn apart by unequal spiritual enlightenment. Even in this fragile beginning God was showing Himself to be true. Together we quickly learned the essential basic tenants to guide our walk. Trinity Broadcast Network made it their priority to expose viewers to the Salvation message as clearly as the gospel sets forth. Many of the evangelical preachers would refer to the writings of Saint Paul who was a Hebrew scholar that persecuted the early converts to Christianity. Paul explains that while proceeding to arrest Christians he himself was knocked to the ground and was blinded by an intense light followed by a vision of seeing Jesus resurrected and alive speaking to him. Out of this comes his complete turn-around where he now proclaims Jesus Christ is the Son of God of whom Paul is now appointed an ambassador and establishes churches to share the good news of salvation for your eternal souls.

A key factor that Paul emphasized can be found in his letter to the church at Ephesus. Ephesians 2:8, 9 states *"For by grace ye are saved through faith, and that not of yourselves, it is a gift of God not of works lest anyone should boast."*

I had always thought that I had to use my will power to keep the Ten Commandments or else I would perish in Hell. But that is not *grace*, that is *works*. *Works* are a personal accomplishment, not a *free gift*.

"Grace" that is amazing!

In his letter to the church in Rome Paul writes *"That if thou shalt confess with thy mouth the Lord Jesus and shall believe in your heart that God has raised Him from the dead thou shalt be saved. For with the heart man believes unto righteousness and with the mouth confession is made unto salvation."* Romans 10:9, 10.

We knew what we needed to do and when TBN announced a revival meeting in our area we attended. When the invitation to salvation was given Roxanne and I walked up to the front and prayed announcing that we received Jesus Christ into our hearts to be our Lord and Savior forever. We were born again! From that moment on we belong to Our Lord Jesus Christ, Amen!

## Chapter Twenty-Three
# SISTER CELESTE

I shared our strange new experience with Lonnie at the hotel while we worked the car park and he invited us to a revival meeting in Opalaka which is on the west side of Miami. Lonnie explained that a woman called Sister Celeste came to the area once or twice a year and held meetings for several nights usually in the ghetto churches there. He continued saying that she always had a deep heartfelt message and that she moved in the gifts of the Holy Spirit. In essence she heard from God in a personal way.

Guidance from above would be a welcomed addition to this new chapter our lives, so Roxanne and I agreed to attend a meeting. Traveling south we passed the warm romantic lights of Miami on our left and continued on into the dark foreboding rubble of decayed buildings and ghetto homes.

We arrived at an old wooden church that was in rather nice condition for the neighborhood and upon entering the building we were taken by the scent of roses and olive oil. Along with the lullaby like singing in tongues, the air was hypnotic. At the altar stood a short firm yet delicate appearing figure of a woman in her forties that had obviously transcended the norm for reality. Her hair was black and her skin was pearl white and glowing softly, and she moved like the wings of a butterfly in her dark blue full length dress.

Celeste's eyes were magnetic black windows to a secret place. You fell into them when they spotted you in the crowd, erasing every hindrance to their knowledge. Celeste's voice was like a panther resting; so full of power and so comfortably inviting. She sang softly praising God in English and in tongues all the while those black search lights passed over and over the congregation like the oars of boat silently stroking a calm lake.

I don't recall today the words she spoke as she began to pray, but I do remember that Celeste spoke to Jesus as if He was right there in the room with her, and she spoke to Him as her beloved. A skeptic might interpret this whole scene as well orchestrated theatrics; with the pleasant odor and the singing, and the way Celeste spoke and moved, but what really would be her motivation for doing so? Was it money or fame? Surely someone with that much talent would pick a safer neighborhood with better financial resources, and that would be anywhere else U.S.A. Celeste had come here from Forty second Street and Ninth Avenue, New York City. This would be a long way to travel just to find more drug addicts and hookers to fleece. No, this was not an act. Celeste was as real as the Beloved One she spoke to, and spoke about.

After she introduced us to her Beloved she began to tell us of His marvelous deeds and His love for us. I had never before seen or heard of such a relationship with this person named Jesus, but I was certain that it was real and that is what was missing in my own life.

When she concluded her message Celeste invited anyone who wished to have this relationship come forward for prayer, and after she prayed with them she began to take some, one at a time, aside by the hand and pray specifically for them off mike. Then Celeste returned to the center of the platform, turned the microphone back on and began to pace back and forth praying and praising the Lord quietly as those searchlight eyes panned across the room. She paused, raised her head and begin speaking back into the microphone "There is someone here who had a nephew or cousin die suddenly, recently. Where are you? I know you are here, where are you? No? I know you are here. I'll get back to you. Now there is a woman here suffering from severe migraine headaches. Come up I want to pray for you."

A tall blonde woman in her early forties arose and walked forward. Celeste tucked the microphone under her arm and prayed for the woman touching her head with an olive oiled hand. She called several more people to her one by one naming specific ailments, abuses or sufferings and always someone responded to her call except for the one who had a nephew or cousin die suddenly.

Celeste called clarifying and insisting "I know you are here. You had a nephew or cousin die recently, suddenly, in a car accident. Come up here I want to pray for you." She waited a few moments and moved on again, Finally she cried out, "Your nephew or cousin, eighteen years old died in a car accident. He hit a wall and the steering wheel punctured his heart. He was chased by the police. Where are you? I know you are here. I want to pray for you."

It was like a splash of cold water on my face! I shuddered astonished and partly I wanted to disappear, but like a child caught hiding in the bushes I reluctantly raised my hand.

"You!" Celeste's index finger pointed to me like the Uncle Sam poster, "Why didn't you raise your hand before? Her deep black otherworldly eyes fixed holding me breathless.

I mumble I didn't know. The crowed chuckled nervously.

"Come up here, I want to pray for you." she spoke evenly.

I complied and Celeste asked me to tell the story. I said I wasn't getting it and then all of a sudden I realized that every word she spoke was exactly what happened to my cousin/nephew Marty who died a month ago in a car accident by hitting the concrete divider on the highway trying to avoid being arrested for having marijuana.

Even this expression "Cousin or nephew" which might seem vague to anyone else was acutely specific to me.

Remember my real cousin Marty with the Corvette that was fourteen years older than me? By now he was divorced from his second wife Ramona, a descendent of a Native American tribe, with whom he had three children; two boys and a daughter Ruthie. Marty's eldest son was named after his grandfather; Marty's dad, my uncle Frank. Cousin Marty's second born son he named after himself, Martin.

Because of our age difference, as Ruthie and the boys grew they often called me Uncle Jim, but also referred to me as their cousin. We all naturally embraced both endearments, but Celeste could never have known this, neither would anyone else in Florida or possibly the world. Only a few of us used the terms interchangeably for each other. If God was trying to tell me something I could trust, this would be like a secrete password. He had to be present in that prayer meeting.

Celeste took a step backward to size me up and down, and with one hand on her hip she announced "You were a drug dealer!"

Covered with shame I lowered my head and with my eyes to the floor I softly replied "Yes."

"You sold drugs to children!" she announced.

"No." I choked out.

"You were a big dealer!"

"Yes." I replied still searching the floor.

Celeste put her arm around my waist then told the congregation that I had met the Lord Jesus and repented, that I was washed in His blood and born again, free from my past. She then said that God's hand was on me and that I would bring souls to Christ.

"You know that you are not going to sit in that pew don't you?" she proclaimed as I shook my head bewildered. Then she said "I'm going to pray for you." and asked for a double portion of the Spirit of Elijah to come upon me.

Celeste returned to South Florida once or twice a year until she went to be with her beloved Jesus in the late 1980's.

*Chapter Twenty-Four*

# BOCA RATON

## *"The Mouth of the Rat"*

All was not well. My new life fit like a cheap tuxedo. I felt all tied up, foolish and out of place, but I determined to continue whatever the cost, and so far it cost me everything I had.

Cosmo had his Real Estate Broker's license hanging on a wall in a building in Pompano Beach that he bought with a nice mature woman partner that I suspected was a little naive to his ways. I needed to plant what little cash I had left after the loss I took on the restaurant deal and I was hoping I could buy a fixer-upper house not too far from the beach in Boca Raton and flip it over after a little work. Cosmo had the listing books and, still owing me money on a past deal he screwed up, this would be one more opportunity to make good by kicking back his commission to me when I bought a listed house through his brokerage. Of course he agreed until the deal was done, then promptly stated that he was in a bind with his partner on their building and needed to buy her out, but would make good on the next one, again confirming his true colors. I would have had to pay another brokerage anyway if I didn't use his company, so I didn't actually lose money with him this time.

People were flocking to Florida and Boca Raton was quickly becoming the new Beverly Hills. I had almost always made money fixing and flipping motorcycles and cars, and almost doubled our money on the house I fixed up in Parsippany. I had always been good at risk taking and now doing only legitimate deals all I had to loose was money; not life or liberty. Plus, I hoped that God was on my side and would honor my efforts.

I purchased a lovely ranch in need of help for $69,000 about five blocks from the beach and tore into it vigorously modernizing the master bath and kitchen with new plumbing, walls, paint, cabinets and appliances. I did all that work myself but hired out the floor tile work and had a contractor install wall to wall carpet throughout the home. I rolled fresh sod on the front yard and Roxanne and I moved in believing for the best. Interest rates were high and with no real job I closed with a mortgage of $1008 per month. That was monstrous compared to the $370 per month we had on the New Jersey house, but I was optimistic.

Parking cars in Hollywood Beach came to an abrupt end when I made a quick turn on the pavement and tore tissue in my knee. We were self-employed parking the cars so there was no insurance to help and I carried none of my own. I lost the job and limped for months. In the meantime I pumped gas in Hollywood Beach at night for five dollars an hour but it almost wasn't worth the trip back and forth. Sure, I applied for jobs but I had no real resume. What could I tell anyone that I had done for the last ten or fifteen years? I had finished real estate school in Florida and obtained a license joining a local real estate office in town, but that paid commission only and I was learning that all the sales came into the masses of subdivisions west of route #95. The builders had their people in-house and weren't taking newcomers. Sure, my property was close to the beach, but it was old and a buyer coming from the north could purchase a similar home brand new for the same money.

Florida was filled with transients and it was quite normal to see hitch-hikers waiting near every highway ramp in the state, and as the saying goes "You can never be too careful" when it comes to picking someone up. This kid couldn't have weighed more than one hundred-thirty pounds and he looked more like fourteen than twenty-one and something told me that if I didn't stop for him he could soon become a statistic. From thirty feet away he was obviously gay and I prayed that I wasn't making a mistake giving him a lift, but I pulled over and Mitch got in my car. He looked weak and tired as he said he was headed to Orlando. He was told it was about an hour up the road. I let him know that he was off by several hours and I was exiting at Boca, but a I'd drop him off a little farther up around West Palm Beach to help him out. He told me that he hadn't eaten in a day and asked would I stop so he could get some water. I could easily see that he had no weapons on his slight frame and no muscle mass either. I was more concerned that he might be HIV positive and was not about to share any water bottle with him, though I didn't have one with me anyway. I kept my bible on the front seat between us.

"There's a Denny's up this way, I'll buy you breakfast." I said knowing I had only six dollars in my own pocket, but that was six more than he had.

Mitch thanked me and explained that he left his mother living Texas a few months ago and hitch-hiked to Florida taking jobs as a waiter but whenever he got a paycheck or a handful of cash he would spend every dime on alcohol, lose his job and move on. We got to Denny's and he asked if I was going to eat. I said I wasn't hungry but for him to order something hoping I would have enough to pay the tab.

Mitch confessed that he would play along with Christians like me to get what he could and that he wasn't proud of it but he wanted to be honest with me. I told him that didn't matter to me. That was between him and God. I'm just filling in the gap.

Two blocks from my house was a Baptist church that had a string of rooms they let out when visitors came to special events. I told Mitch I would put him up for one night at my home and in the meanwhile we would talk to the minister at the church and see if they might help him. He agreed and they gave him a room while he took a job waiting tables at Denny's. A month later he disappeared.

One evening while I was pumping gas in Hollywood Beach a young couple in their twenties with a dog pulled into the gas station in a green station wagon jam-packed with belongings. They were living in the car and bathing at the public outdoor shower at the beach nearby. Tom asked if they could park in the lot and sleep during my shift because they were being chased from the beach at night.

I told them that it wasn't my place but if they left before I closed they could stay this one time.

"That's all we're asking." They said.

I made sure they drove off before I closed up.

They returned on and off during my shift for the next week and we became a little friendly. Now as always I put the gospel between strangers and myself knowing it kept a lot of folks at arms length as in this case, and it always afforded me a safe barrier. Tom and his wife confessed that they were heroin addicts and would go to the clinic in North Miami for methadone.

Roxanne reluctantly agreed and once again I had guests for a week. The pleasure of sleeping in a real bed and using a hot shower offset the temptation to empty my home while Roxanne and I were working. Then the grateful couple and dog moved on.

I took a job building picture frames on Route #1 for about eight dollars an hour but I was not enjoying the "picture" too well. I felt so out of place everywhere.

I had eight grand left and made the tragic mistake of listening to Cosmo one more time. I bought a small single family home one block east of Route #1 in Boca that was both commercially and residentially zoned for $62,500. It had a tenant, that seemed good, but I had to take a second mortgage from the old owner for $10,000 which ballooned in one year. Now I was broke cash-wise and my clock was ticking.

*Chapter Twenty-Five*

# HOLD ON TO YOUR SEET TERRY BOMAR

By now we out grew the church in Hollywood Beach and I began to look for a younger generation to fellowship closer to our home in Boca. My first concern was to find a truly Holy Spirit filled church and hopefully a pastor that I could really talk to. I located the Fifth Avenue Church of God in Deerfield Beach minutes from our house and phoned the pastor for some insight.

"Hello!' he answered with a thick Tennessee accent. "This is Terry Bomar, how can I help you?"

"I'm looking for a bible based Christian church that honestly moves in the gifts of the Holy Spirit." I announced.

"Well, you've come to the right place." The twenty-nine year old pastor replied.

When I asked him what the *Church of God* was about his short answer was, "We're like Baptists with a turbo."

That description fit my needs exactly. Clearly this was a sign from heaven. He continued on explaining that he took over as Pastor about a year ago after the church burned down in a fire. That interested me more. We both saw it as an attack from the enemy and a gift from God. This coming Sunday was Mother's Day and would be my first experience there.

Since the new church had not yet purchased pews, the congregation of about forty sat on metal folding chairs for the time being. As I had done before, I prayed that morning for a sign from God. "If this is where you want me to be please, you have to show me for sure."

Pastor Terry was a trim man of average height with a thick head of almost black hair and moustache that sat above a perpetual smile and a jutting chin. He drank lots of coffee saturated in sugar and preached from his guts as his face sweat rivers that he mopped with a handkerchief in one hand and pointed and waved his long boney fingers with the other, and wow, he was charismatic! This man was born to preach! His message that day was titled "Who Is My Mother?" By the time the first words had left his lips I had to grab the edge of the seat on my folding chair with one hand like a bronco rider and take the full force of a wave crashing into me! I remember describing it as if I was seated directly in front of an open fire hydrant! The sign I was looking for was loud and clear!

The congregation was made up mostly of transplanted southerners in their sixties and above, a very few in their thirties, forties and fifties, and a group of singles in their twenties, as well as infants, children and teens. Again I felt somewhat out of place coming from the north with my bag of experiences that no one could really relate to, and being in my mid-thirties and having never had children of my own, I was having a difficult time being an earthling all around.

*Chapter Twenty-Six*

# MUSCLES

While I was busy exercising my spiritual muscles I was also attempting to put my body in the best shape of my life. I planned a regimen of calisthenics and began jogging every other day. I also dug up an old set of dumbbells with a bench and fit that into my training as well. With the weights and calisthenics your mind is at least partially occupied with counting, but when it comes to running you have to put your head somewhere else to ignore the pain and boredom. Every day I walked my Doberman Kyrie who by now was ten, and used the time away from the house to commune with the God I was seeking and ask His blessings on everyone I could think of. I remembered learning that Socrates paced as he taught and I often observed that all the teachers I gleaned the most from did so as well. I concluded that the brain works best when the blood and oxygen are freely flowing and that the pacing keeps the blood pressure up. Running would of course do the same, but when it came to running I decided to focus only on thanking God for His many blessings one by one. Then concentrated thought should be optimum as well as provide distraction. These became great opportunities to practice memorizing bible versus and poetry and so my memory improved as well as my physical and mental endurance. I was becoming a better man by thanking God for the tools to thank Him with.

Always when I "hit the wall" as runners say when you feel like you can't go on, I would remember something else to be thankful for and so my two miles turned into five and eventually into seven. Florida was hot and I reasoned that running any farther, or any additional exercising could damage my joints or heart or even worse. I decided to seek the knowledge of a professional. So I asked the brightest source I knew to direct me. I asked God. His answer came in the form of an ad in the visible folded page of a newspaper strategically lying noticeably on my dining room table. I never cared for reading the newspaper outside of the auto sales in the classifieds, and haven't since, but I was struck by an add for John DeFendis who held both *Mr. East Coast America* and *Mr. West Coast America* titles offering his services as a personal trainer for an unusually reasonably fee.

*Chapter Twenty-Seven*

# JOHN DEFENDIS

I gave John a call and was amazed at how personable he was. I guess I had a predisposed idea of what a steroid bulked up salesman would sound like. John was nothing like I expected. He has a genuinely compassionate heart for people. We met in his office at Palm Beach Gym where he worked and was currently training to win the Mr. USA title. John was not particularly tall for a body builder, about five foot eight I would guess, but his musculature was otherworldly. He explained that it took about a year of training to put oneself in top competitive form even for a champion, and although he was in the early stage of bulking up his muscle mass for the Mr. USA competition his arms already measured an incredible twenty-four inches around. I stand five foot eight inches and my thighs do not measure twenty-four inches around.

John explained the terms. His fee as a life-time trainer and consultant was $140.00. It included the initial interview from which he designed a customized exercise and diet program for each client plus unlimited one-on-one time, and appropriate program changes as you progressed. A separate reasonable membership charge would be paid to the gym.

I can't say enough about how much John DeFendis helped me grow in every way possible. He is so much more than a bodybuilder and demonstrates a human spirit that eclipses the character and puts most people that I know to shame to this day. In just less than a year

I sat with John and his mom at his Mr. USA Victory Dinner. At that time his mom was all of five foot zero if she was an inch, and probably weighed less than one hundred pounds.

Mrs. DeFendis told me that when John was fourteen years old he came to her and said with assurance "Mom, one day I'm going to be Mr. America."

"John was just a skinny little kid then" she added "but I didn't want to discourage him so I said "Good John, you will, you will." tapping my arm gently and nodding affirmatively. "And look at him now!"

Somewhere I have a signed autograph from John DeFendis stating "Jim, never give up your dreams."

I learned a lot about sets and reps, correct form and concentration, metabolism, diet and nutrition from John.

I invited the Holy Trinity to come and commune with me while I trained and in between sets I would pause and rest for a moment and silently repeat a scripture verse that I had just committed to memory. By adding verses quite often, in time I had an arsenal of scriptures at my immediate disposal and defense, and a well-developed memory as well. I was both armed to defend the gospel and fight spiritual battles. Saint Paul teaches in his letter to the church in Rome that "Faith comes by hearing and hearing (comes by) the Word of God. (Romans 10:17) I knew that I needed a lot of this Word in me to generate the kind of faith necessary to fight my personal battles. For a believer you are always fighting the doubts; the decision you made to believe and obey the Word of God, or that Jesus is the risen Son of God, and beyond that, that God really loves you and will bless and care for you. I felt totally out of place and abandoned all the time. My marriage didn't work, I had no new friends and the old ones from my past thought I was crazy and they were the normal ones on drugs. Plus I couldn't earn a proper living. I humbled myself and tried to gratefully labor. I had the Florida real estate license but it was a commission only game and the builders had the market wrapped up. I took a job in an art gallery in the mall but it paid nothing and was sadly boring. I ran a cash register in a pizza place and eventually put on a suit and became a Maître' D.

I was training myself to believe under pressure.

"God why aren't you prospering me?" I would think, and search my life for secret sins, looking for what might be standing between Him and me. "What could be holding back my blessings?" I remember taking those long walks and praying and trying to show God my willingness to go to any extreme to follow Him. Sometimes I would just drop to my knees in broad daylight hoping no one saw me, offering my life to God to make it into something useful and pleasing to Him. Most of the time "the heavens were as brass" that my prayers could not penetrate. No answer came. On rare occasions I heard the small voice inside beginning with, or accompanied by a scripture. On this occasion I heard Luke 6:47-49.

*"Whosoever cometh to me, and heareth my sayings, and doeth them, I will shew you to whom he is like:*

*He is like a man which built an house, and digged deep, and laid the foundation on a rock: and when the flood arose, the stream beat vehemently upon that house, and could not shake it: for it was founded upon a rock.*

*But he that heareth, and doeth not, is like a man that without a foundation built an house upon the earth; against which the stream did beat vehemently, and immediately it fell; and the ruin of that house was great."*

This parable is taught also in the gospel of Saint Matthew with a slightly different phrasing, but here in Luke's account the additional words "digged deep" rang with special emphasis.

"Digged deep…digged deep…" as I pondered, a still small voice said to me.

"Here's your shovel. Dig." and vanished. I kept running. I kept digging.

I was not going to let anything separate me from the love of God. Periodically I would search my assets in my character as well as my physical belongings for a secret sin or anything that might displease my Holy God. One time I found a socket wrench set that I had since I was a junior in high school. I paid a classmate ten dollars for it and held it dearly ever since, but as I groped backward in my memory it occurred to me that although I had purchased the tools in used condition, deep inside me I had thought that they were likely stolen. I threw them in the town dumpster along with my lovely Sansui 90-90 tuner/amplifier that I purchased legitimately but with money I earned selling pot. Yes I had thought of giving these things to someone less fortunate but my conclusion was that I did not want to receive gratitude that in a sense would honor me for what I once partook in.

I wasn't done digging there. Maybe I was splitting hairs, but I was willing to do whatever needed to be done to be in fellowship with my God. I was searching my heart for hidden idols and my investigation brought me all the way back to Jeananne. Remember, the single most perfectly beautiful drawing I had ever done; the girl in the satin and lace negligee.

Jeananne was a small drawing done on an eight and a half by eleven inch sheet of typing paper nicely matted and framed that moved from a place of proud display to a more modest location as my Christian life progressed. I did not see her as pornographic but certainly sensually as a nude, and I often wondered how my Heavenly Father saw this work from His pure heart with perfect understanding. Did it please Him the way I used His gift to me? We are meant to be beautiful in His sight, made in His image and likeness, made beautifully naked. Will we be clothed in heaven? All things are naked before Him. Yes we will be clothed in His righteousness but will our clothing also be literal? The bible teaches that angels have appeared with clothing and the Son of Man is seen by John in a white garment and a gold breastplate, but are the clothes there because the holy are visiting with the unregenerated?

Also I was concerned that idolatry might be an issue. Anything adored could be spiritual infidelity. The gift to paint so beautifully, the idea of a perfect mate, beauty on any level, and when all is revealed is it simply lust seated on or near the throne of my heart. I would often ask myself if I was trying to fill a hole in my heart where God Himself really belonged.

I prayed many times for clarity about this artwork, and time after time I heard no answer. Then it occurred to me that God was not answering for a reason. He wanted me to decide. I concluded that it was more reasonable for me to remove or destroy something, or some ideal, or affection, even if it was not displeasing, even if it was honorable, rather than have it stand between my God and myself. I also concluded that if God appreciated the drawing then I would see it again in heaven, so with that I took the piece outside to the driveway and removed the art from the frame and setting a match to the drawing, I watched it burn into ashes.

I wasn't looking for anyone's praise for being valiant and didn't plan to tell anyone about these acts of mine. I wasn't sure if they were pleasing sacrifices, or another form of pride. I wanted to practice and demonstrate my willingness to walk by faith in places of uncertainty, painfully if need be.

Someone might see this as self-abuse, as some distorted way of getting attention from a distant Father. Anyway I didn't see angles or hear a heavenly choir or receive some check in the mail or a pat on the back for doing this. I just did what I thought was my best. God doesn't owe any of us anything for turning toward Him or for any act on our behalf. I've been abundantly blessed all through this life so far in many ways some the best of us unintentionally take for granted.

Yet this is not to say that I was at peace with my circumstances. Day by day my resources dwindled away, and like the proverbial widow approaching the unjust judge, day by day I asked God to bless me with an opportunity. Nothing came but the threat of foreclosure and my prayer became another exercise.

Then suddenly one morning when I was at home alone the still small voice answered my request.

"Why are you worried today Jim?"

Calm fell over me and I paused comparing this voice to the one that told me what church to go to in Hollywood Beach, and again to the voice that told me to dig deep. The impression was the same each time.

"I'm listening." I thought with quiet respect.

"Come with me into the living room."

I obeyed silently.

My living room was twenty-two feet long and fourteen feet wide. That was huge for me. It was freshly carpeted and painted, and I had painted the ceiling with a popular textured popcorn finish that sparkled with tiny flakes.

"Look up." The voice spoke softly and paused. "Do you have a roof over your head today?" He asked.

"Yes." I answered not knowing if I spoke aloud or not, though I recall thinking it was a beautiful ceiling.

"Come with me into the kitchen."

I began to feel a little light headed. My kitchen and dining room were adjacent and ran parallel to the whole length of the living room. At the far end I could see my new Kenmore refrigerator. The room receded with my new oven, cabinets and countertop.

I began to feel shame while being led across the length to the appliance. I was told to open it. I felt a little smaller and the voice asked, "Do you have food here today?"

"Yes Lord I do." I whispered reverently. Good healthy food was there.

"Come with me into the bedroom." I was instructed next.

By now I began to quiver increasingly with each step. I knew where we were going to look. My face flushed and my eyes began to tear like rain.

"Open your closet."

We had two separate closets there with sliding doors.

I rolled open my door and pulled the light cord without being told.

"Do you have clothes enough today?" He asked.

I began interrupting "Yes, yes Lord I do. I do have enough!" I cried loud and clearly. "I'm sorry Lord! I'm sorry."

My closet was packed end to end with all sorts of clothing. Maybe nothing brand new, but nothing shameful. Oh yes there were clothes for working in the garage, but there were also beautiful suits and pressed shirts with matching shoes as well.

"Then what are you worried about tomorrow for?" He asked while I recalled Jesus' words recorded in Mathew Chapter 6,

*" Behold the fowls of the air: for they sow not, neither do they reap, nor gather into barns; yet your heavenly Father feedeth them. Are ye not much better than they?*

*...And why take ye thought for raiment? Consider the lilies of the field, how they grow; they toil not, neither do they spin:*

*And yet I say unto you, that even Solomon in all his glory was not arrayed like one of these. Wherefore, if God so clothe the grass of the field, which today is, and tomorrow is cast into the oven, shall he not much more clothe you O ye of little faith?*

*(For after all these things do the Gentiles seek:) for your heavenly Father knoweth that ye have need of all these things.*

*But seek ye first the kingdom of God and his righteousness: and all these things shall be added unto you.*

*Take therefore no thought for tomorrow; for tomorrow shall take thought for the things of itself. Sufficient unto the day is the evil thereof."*
Matt.6:26, 28-34. KJV

This is the challenge to be a Christian. This is faith. This again was my choice, and again I chose to believe Jesus' glowing words.

Still it never "rained pennies from heaven" but I was blessed with an artist's gift. I could paint beautifully. I should be able to make a living creating art.

Many before me have searched the scriptures attempting to understand God's definitions of "prosperity, wealth and blessings" as well as "salvation" and I had been no exception comparing five versions of the Bible: the King James Version, the New King James Version, the New International Version, the New American Standard and the Living Bible. My library grew to include Dake's Annotated Bible, the Matthew Henry's Commentaries, Strong's Concordance and over the years more and more wonderful books and tools some including Greek, Aramic, Hebrew and Latin translations.

Sufficient to say that my own conclusions at the time led me to believe that it was up to me to "dig deep" into the blessings I already possessed and press on with faith.

I had kept the fuel tank and fenders I painted from my award winning motorcycle and after searching the Yellow Pages for business related to art I decided to carry the tank to a local stained glass dealer and see if there might be a related position available.

I plopped my painted fuel tank on the glass counter at Sunrise Stained Glass in Boca Raton and exchanged greetings with Jack Walker and his lovely wife Regina. Jack, a big blue eyed man in his sixties and his petite wife Regina had been in the family glass business here in Boca since their days in New Jersey years ago. They settled in before the building boom in Florida and were well known by the high-end contractors and developers.

"Did you do this with an airbrush?" asked Jack.

"Yes." I replied.

"Have you ever carved glass with a sandblaster?" he continued.

"No sir." I answered.

"Well it is very similar. If you can do this," referring to my paintwork "you can certainly carve glass. It's lunch time. Why don't go home and after lunch put on some old work clothes and come back and I'll show what I'm talking about." Jack said.

"You got it." I replied and headed home with my painted fuel tank.

Upon my return Jack brought me to a sand pile against the north side of the concrete block building. Standing on the ground was an upright cylinder on wheels called a pressure pot which held fifty to one hundred pounds of abrasive sand pressurized with air. Attached to the pot was a compressed air line and a much thicker hose with a cone shaped porcelain tip containing a shut off handle. Jack explained the use of the valves mixing the sand and air and the safety equipment which included thick long-sleeved gloves and a canvas draped face helmet containing a replaceable window.

Leaning a plate of glass against the wall we donned our equipment and Jack demonstrated how to use the cumbersome tool. Similar to using a can of spray paint, though under much higher pressure, the farther the nozzle is held from the glass the larger and less dense a pattern is created. A continuous passing coat will frost the glass. Tarrying in one place carves into the glass. Staying in one place too long and the abrasive sand will burn right through the glass. The slightest burst of sand released toward any unmasked area and the piece is forever marred. There is no room for mistakes.

To make a piece of art you must first clean the glass and cover the entire surface with a vinyl mask sticky side down. The artist's drawing is then transferred by tracing or rubbing the image onto the mask. Then all the transferred lines are traced with a sharp exacto knife. The knife blades dull frequently and must be constantly changed to maintain precision. Even the slightest imperfection will show permanently.

Now the crafter must determine which pieces are to appear closest to the viewer and which should appear farther away. This illusion is determined by the depth and the angle of the cut blast. One by one the puzzle pieces are removed and the section is blasted with sand and air moving at about two hundred miles per hour, each time being careful not to cross over a finished area and thereby blowing away a necessary edge. A misguided burst could burn through a shoe in seconds. Here speed, angle and pressure are important variables with a mind of their own.

Heat from the pressure and friction causes water vapor to saturate your hoses and clots the sand causing spurts, bursts and clogs which require emptying the pot and cleaning the hose, nozzle, and flow valves in the Florida heat. This is a good time to replace the porcelain nozzle as its opening grows wider during use thereby changing the precision of the cut. Besides that the high speed sand particles bounce off of the glass and head directly at the artist willing to sting any exposed skin or eyes. In minutes the returning sand hitting the viewing lens of the helmet causes such frosting that you are reduced to driving in fog, so periodically you slide out the frosted lens and replace it with a clear one from a stack kept not too close by.

Working in the Florida heat fully covered and under a helmet raises your body temperature to dangerous levels and you must constantly remove the helmet and guzzle down bottles of water.

When you feel that the piece is complete you blow it off with air only and examine it for flaws and cracks. Yes cracks! That will ruin your day. Finally you remove the remaining vinyl and clean the piece. Now it will have to be delivered and installed with kit gloves. All this for a lawn boy's wage, but it is art.

Jack executed a few passes on a small unimportant piece and then handed me the gun.

"See what you can do" he said "and I'll return in twenty minutes."

By the time I got a knack experimenting with the cumbersome tool I felt a tap on my shoulder. I shut down the tool and removed my helmet meeting Jack's blue eyes with mine. We both took a breath.

"It took me forty years to learn to do what you just did in twenty minutes." He stated. "You want a job?"

Of course I took the job. It was far from glamorous. It was grueling. I worked in the hot Florida sun in a sand pit staring intently at one piece of glass after another leaning against a white washed wall in a sand storm all reflecting heat and blinding light.

Underneath my helmet I wore a paper particle mask to reduce inhaling the sand dust that got in everywhere including my ears. Between the dust cloud, the frosting lens and the brilliant reflected light I became snow blind, dizzy and dehydrated every day. At night I made line drawings on white paper and worried about destroying my retinas.

Focusing through the fog and dazzling light was exhausting for the eyes so I came up with a method using the outlying rods in the perimeter of my eyes instead of the center cones. The rods are primarily motion detectors mainly in the peripheral vision which are not very good at seeing color, but they do not require a strong pull on the eye muscles to focus as do the cones in the center of your eye. Since this work did not require color detection, only shade, the rods could watch the carved edge changing shape and my focusing muscles could get some relief.

By the end of the day though I would appear to be cross-eyed having to turn my head sideways in order to see forward. This was quite humorous driving home as I watch the expressions on the faces on the oncoming driver passing me by.

"Here comes a crazy man!" I imagined they thought.

Every three months I would quit the job, and after a little time off Jack and Regina would call me back.

It made no sense. My pieces decorated businesses and the homes of the wealthy but I was getting a gardener's wage.

*Chapter Twenty-Eight*

# STILL HORNY AFTER ALL THESE YEARS

Not being able to provide a decent living was an emotional castration for me. Roxanne had not shown any hint of a desire for me sexually in years now and that also contributed greatly to my low self-image. I was a financial failure in the working world and undesired in my marriage. My body on the other hand was fit. I was in the best physical shape of my entire life. Yeah, so that made me horny. When I would pray about that I seemed to already have the answer within, "Love your wife." But I couldn't. I wanted to respect her and provide for her and protect her, but I didn't want to be with her, partly because she showed no interest in loving me as a man. Sometimes I thought it was just manipulative. That she was silently signaling that a man would provide for her and in doing so his reward would be her attention. I became angry, resentful and finally bitter toward her over this. I wanted to be wanted also, not to get crumbs of mercy from her for correct behavior. I wasn't going to beg for something natural and necessary. If she was playing some holdout game it would be to her own loss. We were adults and we were supposed to be following God's will. He would deal with us together or separately. These thoughts I had were my own creation or devil implants, they were immature, selfish attacks on a Godly woman. They were not the truth about Roxanne at all. If

I would have swallowed my pride and approached Roxanne honestly I should have seen the truth, but fear would not let me open my eyes.

Instead, I thought it was too painful for both of us to discuss. I was ripe to shift blame and think "Roxanne had serious traumas from her childhood and her first marriage that were never successfully dealt with. Maybe this was a result of that as well." Whatever her reason for her coolness was, I saw it as "coldness". There was a real schism between us, and I was becoming desperate for some esteem. I had no idea how self-centered I was.

Roxanne now held a manager's position in a chic Boca restaurant called Michael's Palm Cafe' and was able to get me a job there as a maître D because I was attractively fit; what Joe her co-manager called "a clothes horse".

Michael's was frequented by rich Boca socialites, among them were attractive ladies that liked drinking and flirting, a reminder of the life I thought I could put behind me, but wasn't always successful at doing. Now I could add guilt and shame to my very bruised self-image.

At Michael's I also became acquainted with a middle-aged Italian man named Peter Cerrelli. Peter asked if I was an actor looking for work and I explained that I was an artist looking the same.

"Have you ever tried acting?" he asked.

"No," I answered adding "I think many of us secretly imagine it from time to time, but I never pursued the idea."

"Oh!" he said "You would be great, you're a natural."

Peter went on explaining that before he retired he used to manage several artists including Dion Di Mucci back in the doo-wop era having known him from Long Island. Then he told me about a woman called Cherry Faith that ran a course for actors here in Boca Raton.

"You really should give her a try." he suggested earnestly.

"Things are tight Peter, I couldn't afford to take that on right now." I said.

"Would you be interested though? You would be great, I know!" He added "She is running an eight week special right now. I'd be willing to pay for the first group of classes just to get you started. You don't have to reimburse me for it. I can afford it. I'd like to see you get started."

Peter was serious and had no hidden agenda. Maybe this was my opportunity. It wouldn't hurt to try. Lots of television shows and movies were being made in Florida at this time and many of the beautiful people around Boca and the spas and gyms were going on auditions. I joined their ranks and actually got a walk-on part in the final episode of the Miami Vice series.

Cherry Faith was a voluptuous blonde with a sanguine personality. She loved being the center of attention and loved her craft. Professionally trained in the famed Actor's Studio in New York City her colleagues were of notable reputation. Cherry claimed she had dated Rod Stewart for some time and that he proposed to her but she turned him down. When I asked her why she answered, "I don't want to be married to a rock star. I told him I had plans of my own."

In less than a month Cherry told me that I was her star pupil, the best she had ever had the pleasure to work with. At the end of the eight weeks she asked if I would stay on with her without charge. I did for a while but I could see this acting thing was only being tolerated by Roxanne at best. "Though she said she was with me to support me on this, I could see only that she really was not there by her subtle sabotaging." Did I really believe that? And still I had to deal with my own natural desires in the flesh as well as not feeling esteemed by my wife. This vulnerable position bubbled over on occasion and I found myself not just looking but pursuing a fantasy.

I was taking acting classes at another school in Boca and in no time at all I found Patty's eyes irresistible as well as her smile. She was twenty-four. The lust was there with the magic and we glowed for a few weeks. Finally I decided that this was only more pressure on an already crumbling marriage and I withdrew from acting. In truth God was gracious and intervened.

Pastor Bomar called saying that he had a couple at the church that came down from Canada and had lost their life's savings buying a small travel business in Pompano Beach that was a complete scam. Sound familiar?

Bomar said he had a only a few couples in mind that might be willing to put them up for a little while until they made some recovery plans. Roxanne and I took them in under the advice that they not become too comfortable, explaining that the place we were all staying at was disappearing from under our feet as well.

I had lost the rental house I had purchased off of route one some time ago and now we were two months behind on our mortgage payments for the house we lived in. Foreclosure on our home was an imminent threat. I hung my real estate license with a local broker and immediately listed our house for sale. I asked Pastor Bomar and the church accountant to ask the board to consider lending us two months mortgage money which we would pay at the closing on the sale of our home to keep us from foreclosure. The board members voted in favor and we had bought some time.

Statistically a pre-owned home in south–eastern Florida at this time properly priced took an average of eighteen months to sell. I took credit for selling it in two, but it was really by God's grace. We walked away from the closing with zero dollars and no place to live.

We repaid the church, gave away a portion of our furniture and Roxanne found a furnished rental home for us owned by a retired French-Canadian couple. We squeezed into it, but not for long.

## *The Visitor Why?*

Few people kept in touch from my passed life now mostly accepting that I was not returning to my former ways. Cosmo of course was still trying to find ways of bleeding money from whomever he could. Yet oddly Anthony and I still corresponded occasionally. We had some kind of a strange bond. We had not talked about what happened between us years ago and the issue remained an enigma, at least for me.

Anthony had more current problems now. Maybe it was a result of having done so much cocaine in the past few years or maybe it was a combination several things, but now he was addicted to valiums. If you take them while snorting cocaine they counteract the jitters, anxiety, and some of the rapid heart rate allowing for a more comfortable ride, but like with anything mixed with cocaine use including alcohol, it takes continued doses to remain effective. That constant use becomes a problem in itself, and now Anthony was suicidal. That year he had made two extraordinary attempts to end his life. He ended up in a straight jacket in the hospital after the second.

He phoned asking if he could come for a week to get away from the cold and familiarity of the north. I said yes hoping he would find peace in Christ, but it didn't work out that way.

Perhaps as a couple Roxanne and I were not the reflection expected of the divine presence. Perhaps God's presence was less discernable through Anthony's regimen of pills.

Yet Anthony came again with his pills the following year, and on both occasions he proposed this question, "Why should God answer my prayers when He had done so in the past and I abused the gift granted? And beyond that, why should He answer our prayers if He has not answered the prayers for those poor and starving in India and China, the suffering people in the world?"

Anthony was weighing the value of his requests from what he thought would be God's perception.

"I don't know, but I will ask Him that" I replied on both occasions, and in my private prayers I asked God those "why" questions and each time there was only silence.

While Roxanne and I were squeezed into our furnished rented house Anthony and his pills visited us for the third time. This time each one of us was feeling extra stressful and for the third time Anthony asked again "Why doesn't God feed those starving in India? Why doesn't He answer that prayer?"

My lips tightened and my eyes rolled upward, "I don't know, but

I will ask Him again." I spoke, and as soon as the words left my lips I heard the answer.

"Because that's not my job. That's your job and everybody's job that lives here more comfortably than they. I have made provision for everyone. There is food rotting in containers in ports in America that could easily feed the hungry, but you won't see to it! You hold back the bread to drive the price up and you pay the farmers not to grow so much to maintain the scarcity when you should be giving it away and creating a healthy world that has more to offer in return. There is no scarcity! There is an abundance of everything to meet every need! I did my job, you do yours!" and then the voice was silent.

I was silent as well. I was stunned by the answer. Anthony remained angry, and in a few breaths the subject changed to something we hadn't spoken for years about.

"I should have punched you in the face for putting Casey on me!" he blurted out.

"What would you have done?" I returned. " He (my informant) had your name, he knew the layout of my place before anyone else had been there. I brought only you there." I had to find out if my best friend robbed me."

"You want to hit me?" I continued " You still want to hit me after all this time? Go ahead! Hit me if that makes you feel better. Get it off of your chest!"

"No" he answered "I don't want to hurt you." he said as he lowered his head waging it slowly side to side. We waited for the adrenaline to subside then he reached out to shake my hand in a gesture of peace. I gripped his hand and the moment passed like a bad dream. We never spoke of it again.

## *Why?*

By now I was beginning to understand what it would cost me to be a Christian, what I would forgo, and what I would leave behind.

Loneliness was always a part of my life anyway, but it was hard to believe in the benefits. Eternal life was hopefully for the future, and being in better health was a reality, but having no tangible future in this life and no intimacy in marriage or with my family, or anyone at all was gnawing at my soul. A part of me would almost do anything to soothe that ache. I longed for a real fulfilling relationship, and however I tried I could not connect to Roxie, or even communicate the need to her. I was in between a rock and a hard place. To stay together or separate; we would lose either way. By staying was I being noble, or was that just being a coward? I did not know. Would leaving be selfish, a sinful lack of faith? From what I read it would seem so. In any case I was not going to leave Roxanne without a home, a penny or a plan for her income and safety. If I was working, if I had some self-esteem, would these questions diminish? "Why was there no clear opportunity for the talents God gave me?"

## Why?

On top of this our Canadian landlords gave us notification that our lease was soon up and that they would be coming down to occupy the house themselves. It was time for us to move again. With our remaining belongings packed under the carport I clipped a leash onto Kyrie, and as always, prayed for the answers as we walked.

"God, you gave me this talent. I am your artist. Why won't you give me an opportunity to use it to care for my family? What do you want me to do now? We have no place to live."

I had made maybe ten paces from the end of the driveway and those words I prayed had just left my mind when I looked up to see Pastor Bomar leaning his head out of the driver's window following his left arm.

"Hey Jim!" he called through his huge smiling face. "How's it going?"

I rolled my eyes toward heaven and smiled back. Bomar's joy was contagious.

"You see all my belongings pilled-up in the carport behind me right?" I answered matter-of-factly.

"Well that's what I was just going to talk to you about. I was wondering if you might consider something."

"I was just talking to God" I said. "What do you have in mind?"

"Would you consider teaching art as an elective one or two days a week in an Accelerated Christian Education program run by our church at our recently acquired building on Pompano Beach?"

"Yeah I would but I really need a place to live right now." I explained.

"Well that's good because there's an apartment on the third floor that looks right out on the ocean and you can have a large private art studio next to your classroom on the second floor that has the same huge ocean view too! Now if Roxanne would consider running a Christian Day Care across the street from the school the church will pay her a salary and if you teach only two classes a week we will give you the art studio for yourself as well as the apartment on the third floor with your utilities covered as well!"

Of course we took the deal and moved into a fifty room school building that had an Olympic sized pool as well in the courtyard with gated access.

The school, along with another two story building across the side street, had originally been a private academy which had closed its doors some years before. It belonged to a member of our church who was still paying property taxes on the empty buildings year after year. Visionary Pastor Bomar had dreamed of having a Christian school now he had a wonderful opportunity to do so. The property owner could offer the church the use of the buildings for only the cost of the repairs and upkeep, and receive in return a forty-five thousand dollar tax savings for his contribution of the property use. Now the buildings along with one of the two Olympic swimming pools would be maintained, occupied, and less likely to be vandalized. Everyone was a winner.

I remember the first time I lifted the lever that opened the seven foot wrought iron gate that accessed the courtyard and pool, and walked the adobe block pathway toward the entrance to the cafeteria. The hinges squawked loudly as I began to silently ask God "Why would you have me teach your children?"

"Because I trust you." He replied.

"You trust me…with your children?" I returned amazed.

"Yes, with my children." He answered assuredly.

It was more than a pat on the back. I felt worth for the first time since I could remember. "God trusts me…with His children!" I said to myself taking a long breath and, feeling as if my body got lighter, I quickened my pace toward my new nest above the ocean.

Three flights of stairs may have been a healthy challenge for me at the time but for Kyrie my Doberman, they were a painful reminder that her hips were wearing out. I would often take her on the beach in the evening and throw a piece of drift wood for her to retrieve but now she began to fall in the sand. Kyrie was so stout hearted that she amazed me. One evening in the dim light of dusk she returned with a much larger branch dragging from her mouth. It had to be two inches in diameter and four feet in length. It was awkward but she was determined to bring it all the way home. I opened the rear gate to our building and Kyrie dragged the log onto the cement staircase and began her trek up the three flights. Twice she collapsed on the stairs but she would not abandon her mission. Sadly she reminded me of Jesus falling with his cross, and lifting himself up to finish His work on it.

Not long after she began losing bowel control and one morning I awoke to find her curled up in our closet breathing hard as water droplets blew from her nose. She weighed about seventy pounds but I gathered her gently up into my arms and managed the three flights or stairs putting her on the rear seat of our Pontiac and Roxie and I drove her to the veterinarian. Kyrie had a heart attack.

We watched the young doctor inject Kyrie with something that instantly stabilized her and then with two needles fine-tuned her levels as he spoke to me.

"Kyrie had a heart attack and these drugs will hold her until they wear off and then she may be able to be treated, but my experience is that most often once the drugs wear off she might be stabilized one more time with them, but even then usually they ( dogs) have another attack and can't come back. I know you love her and I'm doing all I can but I feel you must be prepared for the inevitable."

This was too much for Roxanne to watch plus she was needed at the Day-care so I decided to drive her back there and come right back to clinic to be with Kyrie.

Kyrie passed in the moments before I returned.

## Chapter Twenty-Nine
# EZEKIEL

Two weeks rolled by sadly as Roxanne and I mourned Kyrie, then one evening Anthony called out of the blue. He asked about Kyrie knowing she had been suffering and I informed him that she had passed.

"Are you thinking of getting another dog?" He asked with a hopeful voice.

"No." I explained. "I don't have a real home for one or especially the time and patience to raise another from a puppy. Plus I'd be real selective and particular about what I would like in another, and that would equate to spending a lot of money that I don't have right now. And again, it would be unfair to ask another dog to fill the place that Kyrie left."

"Come on," said Anthony, "you are a dog guy. You always had a dog. When's the last time you were without a dog? Another dog is just what you need to heal the pain."

I reiterated my position.

"I'll give you Zeke."

"Zeke?" I enquired.

"Yeah, Ezekiel actually."

"That's a biblical name." I replied.

"Yeah, he is a really unique animal. He needed a unique name." Anthony said and continued explaining the creature's genetics and training.

Ezekiel was a hybrid; a cross of two pure breeds, no more. Once a third breed is added you get a "mixed breed" or what is commonly called a "mutt". A Doberman Pincher is actually a hybrid, a combination of Rottweiler and Manchester Terrier. Once the blood lines were established this hybrid became accepted as a pure breed.

The advantages of creating a hybrid are that the relationship tends to reproduce only the best characteristics of each breed, and the new creation is most always stronger, lives longer and is often larger than both parents.

Pure breeds over time tend to become too closely related and this weakens the genetic pool. Another advantage of hybrids is that by bringing in outside blood lines, these imperfections and weakness get washed out.

Ezekiel is the product of valued blood lines of both champion Greyhounds and champion Pit Bull Terriers.

Anthony went on to explain that Ezekiel, now fourteen months old, was fully obedience trained on and off the leash, with both verbal and non-verbal commands. He was socialized and not attack trained so that his activities and appearance were not threatening in the public arena. Anthony did warn me that Ezekiel did possess tremendous speed and power and apparently found it humorous on occasion to run full speed crisscrossing your path until he had you confused as to what direction he would be coming from and then throw himself sideways into your legs and knock you right off of your feet! Anthony claimed Zeke once slammed him so hard that he knocked the wind out of Anthony embarrassing him in front of a crowd of onlookers.

Anthony explained that he had a buyer for Zeke in the city for seven hundred dollars but that he wanted to be sure his dog had a good home with someone he knew would truly care for him. As I began to explain that I could not afford the cost of airfare let alone buy the dog Anthony insisted that he wanted to give Zeke to me and that not only would he pay for the flight, but that the dog would be accompanied by a medical record including all his up-to-date inoculations, a new sizable comfortable crate, and instruct me over the phone as to all his obedience commands.

I agreed to talk it over with Roxanne and with her blessing we met our new buddy at the airport. Ezekiel was the most precious and wonderful gift. I could not have imagined the joy that beautiful animal brought to us for the next fourteen years.

## *School Lessons*

Because our enrollment was small covering a wide variety of ages it made best sense to divide my art classes by age into two groups by of about twenty students each. I created my own lesson plans and demonstrated them on the black board, laying my images out in detail the night before class. I also filled in often for Pastor Robin Tripp who doubled as teacher and Principle, when he was either absent or overloaded with his many responsibilities under Pastor Bomar. This often included being the Physical Education teacher, teaching a boy's character building class and taking turns with Roxanne and Robin driving the kids to gymnastics classes at another school.

Bus driving had its moments, particularly when tooling down Route 95 on a class fieldtrip to the Miami Zoo which I organized for the art classes, but my bus driving carrier really peaked on a routine trip to gymnastics.

As I prepared to load up our school bus with the students heading for gymnastics Roxanne informed me that she had used the bus the day before with the daycare kids and all went well but she recalled a squeak coming from under the hood when she shut the motor off. Sound familiar? I asked her if the bus appeared to have lost any power or made any smoke and she answered "No." adding that it appeared to be fine. So I opened the engine cover and checked the oil and everything seemed to be okay so I closed the hood, climbed in and started the engine. The gauge showed plenty of oil pressure and I saw no smoke in my review. There was no lifter tap or any sound out of the ordinary. I read the faces of Pastor Tripp and Miss Roxanne; as she was generally known, and we were all in agreement that the bus was fine. After all the church had the bus's 454 cubic inch Chevy big block engine completely rebuilt only a year ago.

The kids piled in and in the first row behind me sat Johnny and Susan Timbrell, a couple of quiet chubby blue-eyed Irish kids whose parents spoke with a charming brogue.

We pulled away from the school and crossed the causeway bridge and began heading north on Federal Highway, the main business road.

"She sure sounds good Mister Walsh!" offered Johnny smiling up at my rearview mirror.

"They always sound their best right before they blow!" I said smiling back in my mirror. The motor was humming along in agreement when suddenly it exploded with a loud bang. Immediately the entire bus filled up with blue smoke and in my outside mirror I saw a piston and connecting rod tumbling behind us in a cloud of smoke. Fortunately the children stayed seated, probably in shock from the blast, and the traffic all came to a carful stop allowing me to steer the bus into a parking lot off to the right. The kids were delighted to use the rear emergency door as well as exiting up front, and performed like little soldiers without panic.

Once I had them all accounted for and lined up at a safe distance from the smoldering bus, and informed the school which sent a posse of minivans, I decided it was safe to satisfy my curiosity and open the hood again. Some of the boys could not resist as well and hurried behind me to view the damage.

Looking down at the motor I could easily see the pavement below. There was a hole the size of a soccer ball in the engine block where the missing piston had launched from. I decided that the squeak that Miss Roxanne heard was a dry rod bearing that eventually seized to the crankshaft forcing the connecting rod to break in two and send it flying with the piston through the engine. We all agreed that it was really cool blowing up the bus, especially since no one was injured.

## Angie and Lenny

Two of my students in particular showed great artistic promise. The Grajalas family consisted of a widow mom; Petra, and her children; three boys, and one girl; Angelique. Lemuel who was twelve was the youngest member and had always displayed a talent for drawing. Unlike Lenny who was often seeking attention, Angie, at fourteen was cool tempered and soft spoken, lovely and ethereal. Her deep alto voice was always a resonate whisper, a windy breath that sounded more like the sea speaking; befitting her name; Angelique. I immediately adopted them both.

Not so surprisingly Angie turned out to have an excellent gift for drawing and painting.

Petra and her family originally came from Puerto Rico and were deeply rooted in their Christian faith. Her brother Juan Ortiz had been a pastor in Massachusetts years ago and was now building custom staircases in expensive homes here in Florida. John and his wife Judy had three daughters and a son; Johnny. Johnny and his younger sister Marnie also attended the school where I was teaching.

## A True Sage and Mentor

Petra and Juan had wonderful spiritual insight and my favorite memory of Juan is sitting at his dining room table drinking thick espresso and chewing on chunks of sugar cane he shaved from a stalk that leaned against the wall in his dining room. The caffeine and sugar kept us going for hours as Juan opened windows of spiritual mysteries I was eager to fathom. Like his niece Angie, Juan had a magical voice that hypnotized and transported the listener, and his laughter was medicine. His insights guided and strengthened my faith, increased my knowledge and nurtured my hope in the things of God.

Still, I was not about to become a monk. My view of the ocean was speckled with lovely girls wearing thongs while my marriage was frostbitten. I try to believe Our Lord will fix this too.

*Chapter Thirty*

# BOCA HOTEL MURALS

In the Springtime of 1989 the eminent Boca Hotel and Country Club had begun renovations, and fortunately for me a young woman from our church held an office job there. When Lynn heard that the management was looking for an artist to decorate some exterior walls, she relayed the information to me to see if I would be interested in the work. All the members of the country club are millionaires and though the hotel would be prudent in negotiating such construction contracts they were certainly solvent and trustworthy debtors. Being informed of my interest Lynn proceeded to tell Ed Brophy, the Resident Manager that she knew a capable artist willing to examine the project. We made an appointment and after navigating through the hotel's security I met with Mr. Brophy at his office in the hotel. Ed explained that he wanted tropical plants painted on the exterior of some of the private cabanas on the beach and also on two lengthy temporary construction walls that protected hotel guests from the sight and sounds of the improvements being done on the opposite side. The delightful and well-spoken manager made it clear that he was in charge here and that he would only consider realistic pricing.

I was confident as I showed him my portfolio and explained my design and approach to accomplish the desired result. Mr. Brophy was obviously impressed.

We easily came to an agreement and he handed me the keys to

the kingdom which included a pass to access the hotel, the manager's private parking spot, my own cabana and towel service, plus use of the outdoor hot tub and beach as well as free lunch daily.

Guests were complimenting my work, as well as my physique, to the management. One guest mistook me for a middleweight boxer. It seems that the past few years in the gym were paying off. Ed liked hearing the reports and asked me to stretch out my time there because he said that it was good for the hotel. He also asked me if I could do something with the fire extinguisher boxes located along the cabana walls. They were receded like medicine cabinets with a glass door allowing the red extinguisher to be blatantly visible. I suggested that I would continue my faux foliage that included tropical trees with branches reaching through the boxes and then I would sandblast a toucan lighting on a branch on the glass cover. Some of the glass would remain clear while the frosted bird image would still allow enough red from the fire extinguisher to be visible in keeping with the fire codes.

With the job completed and full payment made Ed asked me to come up with an idea for some large glass walls that would break the wind from the beach while still exposing the view from their Italian Grotto café.

I proposed to blast the statue of David and other famous Italian renaissance pieces into movable safety glass panels.

At Mr. Brophy's request I produced a comprehensive drawing and left it for his approval.

After one week Mr. Brophy called saying that the outdoor grotto project was cancelled, and also that he was apologizing for damaging my drawing. It had been left by a potted plant and when the plant was watered the vase leaked onto the carpet and my rendering had soaked up water like a sheet of cardboard.

At first I shrugged it off and retrieved my drawing, but it began to upset me that the hotel did not even offer to compensate me. I called Ed about it and he became livid saying that he had done me a favor employing me and that he would pay for it but we would never do business again. I should have accepted payment as respect for my work but I let the matter die.

## Fly Fishing

I did not hear very often from my brother John living in New Mexico with his wife Carole, and their three daughters, unless he was anxious about something. This time he called me explaining that he was in a partnership with three other men owning a used car business and they were having financial trouble. On asking my advise, I replied that "Honesty is always the best policy." and by being honest, anything can be truly worked out.

John took this opportunity to invite me to come to New Mexico and visit with his family adding that he would like to take me fly fishing. It was in fact my brother who taught me how to fish when we were children and I had not had a pole in my hands since then. Fly fishing is a whole other thing. It is an art form.

When I arrived, John brought me to an auto auction and we picked out a used Mercedes Benz which he purchased for his car lot but gave me the use of while I was there. He also brought me to a local gym knowing my workout habit and said he would consider buying this small business if I was willing to work it explaining that the current owner changed his mind daily about selling the little gym and vitamin store, as well as the selling price.

We went for haircuts where I met Pam Benson who cut my hair and I took a photo of her.

Finally John hired his friend who was a fishing guide, and we suited up and went off to the San Juan River fly fishing for trout. We all caught fish. John was amazing and of course caught the biggest and the most, but I had a perfect moment. I mean it was a day to always remember. I finally had my brother as my own brother, and it was wonderful there in the land of enchantment. I remember almost hearing Tom-toms echoing off of the canyon walls.

When I returned to my studio in Pompano Beach I made a colored pencil portrait for Pam and sent it to her, and I made two large acrylic paintings for John and his family, one painting of his two oldest daughters, Leah and Dana, wearing sun glasses, and one large dessert landscape.

It would be years before we would see each other face to face again.

*Chapter Thirty-One*

# ART INSTITUTE

I decided to use my extra time wisely. The Art Institute of Fort Lauderdale was close enough to commune and I always wanted to finish school. Perhaps going there would open more doors for me.

I prayed for a sign. I still wasn't convinced that I truly was an artist. Now I would have professionals critique my work.

I felt awkward being close to two decades older than the other new students but we all had a common denominator; artistic talent and a desire to develop and utilize it.

Our classes were large as we sat elbow to elbow while Professor Mike Carnegie assigned our first lesson.

"Select any item from your art box and render it once in pencil, once stippled with a rapidograph pen, and thirdly cross-hatched in pen and ink."

The following week we tacked our completed drawings on the wall side by side and Professor Carnegie selected them one by one and gave critique. Silently I prayed for a sign.

For a while he commenced in order from left to right. My work was about fifth from the far end so I assumed it would be some time before he got to it. I was right, but surprisingly when it finally looked like it was my turn Mike tapped the wall below my art with his index finger twice and said, "I will come back to this one." and moved on to the next. It was beginning to look like a sign from God since Mike dramatically saved my artwork for last, but it became crystal clear with his critique.

"There are great artists and there are great illustrators, but on rare occasions there are both qualities in one person. James is one of those." Professor Carnegie continued explaining the values of my work and ended his critique with "I would hang this piece of art in my home."

I managed to continue in school into my third semester maintaining a 3.92 GPA but problems arose within the church leadership and with only one week's notice our school and day-care would close. This was the end of the second year there and Roxie and I would again be homeless, and jobless as well. With no warning we had to put our belongings into a storage unit and give most of our remaining furniture away.

*Chapter Thirty-Two*

# TIME TO MOVE AGAIN

Pastor Bomar stepped down and Pastor Robin Tripp and his wife Debbie with their two children took us into their home. They were really great to us but it was difficult for me to feel at ease in someone else's home. In a short while Roxanne was able to get us into a condo on West Lauderdale for gratis owned by non other than her former husband's brother; Carl. It was close to route 95 so I could get to the Art Institute easily and it was close to a public school yard where I could run Zeke in the evenings. One time Zeke found a soccer ball to play with and quickly I learned that my dog could open his jaws wide enough to actually carry the ball around full of air. Of course eventually his large canine teeth punctured the ball and his task became easier.

I found a gym close by as well and I trained there with my friend Dottie whom I dubbed *Dottie the Body*, who was preparing for a body builder competition.

Living in the x-brother-in law's condo was not an ideal situation for Roxanne or me so we stayed there for less than a year hoping for a break. When Carl informed us that he would be coming down to use the place we were taken in by Ann Billings, a woman from our church that had a full sized female poodle. Roxanne and I slept on a pull-out couch and I played with Zeke in a lot across the street.

Ann's home was small and the confining situation became unbearable.

When my mother asked how we were doing during our telephone calls I related that I had nothing left and nowhere to go. She agreed to take us in and I left Roxie and Zeke at Ann's and returned to the home I had grown up in, in New Jersey. I was hoping that things would work out for Roxanne and myself separately, but I was not going to abandon her if she wasn't finding some success there either, and although I enjoyed this time apart, I kept the door wide open for her to return also. Within a month Roxanne and Zeke said farewell to Florida and made their way back to Mom's as well.

The year now would be 1992 and I would be forty years old. I close this recollection of the events of my life here as I look again at the crossroads. Perhaps this is not the safe harbor we had expected but it is necessary to catch one's breath for a moment, and just honor God for giving each of us our own unique and marvelous lives, before taking you with me through the next twenty years of my yearning and learning experiences.

I began writing this book ten years ago. I was fifty-one years old. I am sixty-one years old at this juncture. A whole world of exciting and dangerous things have happened in the twenty-one years that I haven't yet revealed to you. That will be in the next section. I will give you this though, Roxanne and I are still together and in love with each other following the sweet scent of our Master Jesus Christ. We are happy.

# THE END

www.ingramcontent.com/pod-product-compliance
Lightning Source LLC
LaVergne TN
LVHW091547060526
838200LV00036B/733